HEALTH CARE IN THE TRENCHES

HEALTH CARE IN THE TRENCHES
by Jimmie K. Butts

CHAPEL HILL
PRESS, INC.

Published by The Chapel Hill Press, Inc.
1829 East Franklin Street, No. 300A
Chapel Hill, NC 27514

ISBN Number 1-880849-60-7
Library of Congress Catalog Number 2003104613

Printed in the United States of America
07 06 05 04 03   10 9 8 7 6 5 4 3 2 1

I dedicate this book to my grandchildren, Jason, Jennifer, Kevin, Tyler, Michael, Sara, and Hayden. With your busy lives, someday you may want to read of your Mimi's adventures in the trenches.

I also have a few words of wisdom for you, based on lessons I have learned in this seventh decade of my life. They have to do with the people in your life:

> Honor and respect those who have led and
> taught you and gone before you.
>
> Gently lead those who may follow you.
>
> Most important, appreciate those who
> walk beside you and are your friends.

With special appreciation to Edwina, Jeff, Stephanie, and Misty, all of Chapel Hill Press, for the encouragement, guidance, and support to finish *Health Care in the Trenches*.

Contents

Preface

As a child, I would sit near either of my grandmothers and listen to her tell stories. I loved to hear the stories of the way things used to be when they were children. I followed each of them into her individual kitchen and watched her cook. Finally, my Mama Kennedy taught me to make biscuits on the Hoosier cabinet that stood in a little hall between the kitchen and the dining room. Even when the other grandchildren would go out to play, I seemed to prefer listening to the stories.

When I became a teenager, I would visit them and help with simple chores, sweep the porch, do their hair, wrap Christmas presents. I even told my Mama Kennedy about my boyfriends. She would quote the Scriptures to me and give me advice, which I did not always take. I loved both of my grandmothers, Mama Kennedy and Mama Walker (my mother's mother), very much. Mama Walker was the more mystical, superstitious, and mischievous of the two.

There was another grandmother in my young life, my great-grandmother, Mammy Brock, my fathers' grandmother. She and my great-grandfather, Pappy, always lived with Mama and Papa Kennedy. They were a comforting presence. I never heard them complain, and they were always treated with respect by even the rowdiest members of the family.

Pappy walked every weekday selling Watkins Products to the neighbors. These were everyday household products, from brooms to vanilla flavoring. He was tall, erect, and (to me) looked like a Native American with his high cheekbones and dignified persona. Mammy loved to go, go, go. When an uncle or anyone said, "Mammy, I'm going to the store. Do you want to go with me?" before the words were finished, Mammy had her hat and pocket book and was ready to go.

I suppose that the influence of these fine women filtered down to me in a couple of ways. I love "to go." Anytime someone suggests that we go somewhere, I start making plans. There is a wanderlust that seems to be inherited. And I love to tell stories. For years, I have been on the professional-speakers' circuit telling stories, mostly funny, to entertain and inspire my audiences. Now I have another story to tell. This book is a collection of stories of my travels as a *locum-tenens* (medical Latin for "temporary substitute") nurse practitioner. During the course of every assignment, I wrote a diary or journal to record events, experiences, the people I met, and the landscape of the places I have been. I suppose that those grandmothers have influenced me more than I realized. There are other important people in my life who have encouraged my whimsies, my playfulness or sense of humor, and confidence. Today, I want to thank my grandparents for their love and encouragement. I also want to thank all those who make it possible for me to follow my dream, those who have kept the home fires burning, and those who have helped me to write about my experiences.

Introduction

Many have asked me why I chose to try my wings after the age of sixty. There is no simple answer. As a young woman, I was not encouraged to go to college—my family didn't have the money, but no one told me that I could get a loan or a scholarship. I accepted the notion that a female high school graduate could get a husband, have babies, and her life would be complete; what more could I possibly want? I had no role models to inspire me and had no idea that I had abilities and attributes that could lead to a successful career as a professional of any kind.

I discovered that I could attend a diploma program and become a registered nurse in three years and that it would only cost me six hundred dollars. I took a job as an editorial assistant for a tiny publishing company in Nashville, Tennessee, my hometown. I lived at home with my parents and saved money out of my monthly salary of $150; I applied to Mid-state Baptist Hospital School of Nursing and began classes in the fall of 1954.

I had fallen in love, as schoolgirls often do, but it seemed that marriage was not in the picture at that time. I also had a very strong faith in God and asked for guidance about my future. Once I moved into the Campus House on the hospital grounds, I knew that it was the right place for me. I loved every minute of the experience. The freshmen were bussed to Belmont College for our didactic classes, Chemistry, Anatomy and Physiology, Biology, and English.

Although we were not in the mainstream of the college's academic life, I was excited about the journey on which I was embarking.

Am I rambling? There are two points that I want to make. First, becoming a nurse takes more than a classroom experience and the right scientific courses. Today nurses are well paid, well educated and very professional. Yet, they are leaving the field in droves. Why? I think many of them have gone into the field for the wrong reasons. Was it for the good salary? Was it to meet a nice doctor, get married, and use their skills to be good mamas? Did they follow their hearts? Did they have a fire in their bellies? Medicine requires a passion for the work, a fire in one's belly!

I had that passion, but I had another passion. I fell in love again, married before I finished school, and within two years, our first child was born, followed by two others. Despite the fact that no one could have loved my wonderful husband and my three children any more than I did (and do), there was smoldering desire in my soul to follow a new path. I talked with my husband about going back to work and weathered my in-laws' disapproval. And my husband encouraged me to follow my dream. Sure, the extra money helps, but by the time you pay for a second car, someone to help with the housework and children, it is not the paycheck that makes a significant difference.

When our children had grown and were on their own and my husband had retired, the old restlessness returned. I had the most coveted position as manager of the SAS Institute Health Care Center and earned a good salary and benefits, yet I longed to go places where other nurses did not care to or have the freedom to go. Once again, I am still married to a man who was aware of my desire to try my wings. My arguments were evidently convincing. So I started taking temporary assignments that averaged about two months each (sometimes longer and mostly shorter) and could then come home to do my "retirement" thing.

This book is for all of those who supported me in following my dream. It is also for those of you who desire to (What is it they say now?) "step outside the box," stretch yourselves, and reach for the stars.

The second point is to share with you the *art*, as opposed to the "science" of nursing. Like every art, it seems to be elusive, constantly in search of definition or meaning in the healthcare field today. Is it because the high-tech aspects of today's healthcare demand all of a nurse's time? I have been hospitalized a number of times in my life, and as a patient, I have discovered that a nurse is rarely at your bedside anymore. Therefore, the opportunity to become the kind of nurse who finds true happiness in his or her work seems limited by the time and knowledge it takes to keep up with the large amount of documentation that is required today. As a result, many nurses leave looking for something more personally gratifying, which in some cases also offers a larger paycheck.

I believe this is also true in any business setting. We are a generation of highly paid professionals who can lose sight of the intrinsic rewards of our work when they are caught by what I call the "golden handcuffs": high salaries, promises of profit sharing, luxurious benefits beyond the health-insurance benefits that are being reduced in every type of business. Where is the passion for the work or careers we have chosen? As I write this, those high-tech industries that offered promises of high incomes, etc., are falling like dominoes. Talented employees are being laid-off systematically, losing not only their jobs, but also their health insurance and their hopes of rewarding and comfortable retirements.

How fortunate for me that I have work that I love and can continue to contribute to the field of nursing. It is not because of the scientific or clinical aspects of the work that I remain in the profession. It is because of the *art* of what I do is so rewarding.

As Ricky Ricardo would say to Lucy, "Let me essplain, Lucy." In medical science we have clearly defined formulas for diagnosing and treating a patient. In another ten years, patients will probably be able to turn on a computer, fill out questionnaires about their health and after certain laboratory tests, blood work, electrocardio-grams, etc., the proper diagnoses can be printed out and plans of treatment will appear on the screen. Recently a friend of mine went to the Veterans Administration clinic for a "physical." The health-care provider, who happened to be a physician's assistant (PA), never looked at the patient. Questions appeared on the screen of the computer, and the PA recorded the patient's answers. A formula appeared advising that the patient's medicines be changed to better control his blood pressure, and the PA prescribed them for him. Although the patient had some questions about some skin prob-lems, they were never addressed. In fact, he was never even asked to remove his clothes, and he was actually relieved that he did not have to have a physical examination.

I see physicians who use the computer to document the assess-ment of a patient, but, thank God, they still look me in the eye and do the appropriate examination. In each practice, hospital, clinic, and office setting, the skill to use a computer seems to be more highly valued than the ability to perform an actual examination of the patient.

My journeys during the seven years I was on the road convinced me, more than ever, that one must perfect the *art* of caring for peo-ple. This is true if you work in any field. The *art* of which I speak has to do with the observational skills that are being lost. The *art* of nursing requires active listening, looking into a patient's eyes, look-ing and touching a patient's body, and honing the skills that one needs in order to understand who the person is and what he or she is all about.

My computer skills are so basic that they are at what is really the kindergarten level these days. In fact any of my grandchildren can do things with a computer that I don't even want to think about. I call on them to turn on the cable TV or the VCR and work my cell phone.

But I know how to talk to people, whether they are patients or my grandchildren, and how to connect with the many questions they may have. I know how to listen with my heart as well as my ears. I could employ those same skills as a shoe salesperson. In fact, I may be a shoe salesperson some day. (Well, maybe that isn't such a good idea, since I'd probably spend all of my paycheck on shoes.) And if I were, each of my customers would leave with a sensible well-fitting shoe after a pleasant encounter with me. But today we frequently just go into a store where we find our own shoes, look for the right size and style, and hope we will be happy with our choice.

And those of you who are ladies: have you tried to buy a bra lately? Where are the clerks? They are at the computerized checkout stations. There used to be saleswomen who helped you find the right fit and style and would bring more bras to the dressing room so that you did not have to dress each time you needed to go back to the racks and search for another style or size.

There are some who still assist customers in the old ways, but one must look for them. Darlene Gardner runs "Lovely Lady," a store in Cary, North Carolina, that caters to women who have had breast cancer. She is the ultimate salesperson, one who thinks more about her clients than her paycheck. Those of us who have had breast cancer know the value of the personal touch in her business as she fits bras for our altered breasts or finds just the right wig for clients who are undergoing chemotherapy.

I hope you will see, through my experiences, that connecting with people, whether they are patients, customers, family, or co-workers by listening, touching, laughing, and caring, with your eyes, ears, and heart can make a difference. The rewards for you are priceless. I am no Mother Teresa. I have been paid for my endeavors. The rewards go beyond that, however, when I see the twinkle in the eyes of the aged and the wonder in the eyes of a child.

You'll see what I mean. Now, let's get started...

Here I Go!

In April 1994, I arrived in Bethel, Alaska. Bethel certainly did not look like the travel brochures I had seen of lovely, mountainous Alaska. The land was barren and flat, covered with snow, and the wind was blowing furiously. I wore a dress, the likes of which no one around there had seen for a number of months, I was sure. When the plane landed, I walked down the steps into that cold wind, and my skirt flew almost over my head, erasing every trace of dignity I had mustered. The airport terminal was a big metal barn, and there was no nice covered walkway to get from the plane into the building.

I had called from Anchorage to make sure that someone would meet me, since the evening was fast approaching and arriving after dark made this adventure feel a little more treacherous than I wanted. The building was filled with people dressed in big wooly coats, hats, and boots, and the only way I could tell the guys from the gals were the beards. I finally heard a big man say that he was "looking for a Jimmie Butts." I was quick to inform him that Jimmie was here in the flesh. He was also there to pick up another nurse who was returning from a weekend in Anchorage. We piled our luggage into his muddy little station wagon and made our way to the compound.

The compound consisted of the hospital and adjacent living quarters for the personnel. I had spied the hospital from the air. It truly looked like a "yellow submarine." I was excited and anxious to make my nest, so to speak.

When we departed from the "terminal," I saw the mud, mud, and more mud—black, not red like our North Carolina tar-heel mud. The compound's apartments were adequate and clean, but sparse. My room was the largest. There were two other rooms on the second floor with mine, but their doors were closed, and the place was quiet. There was little evidence that anyone else lived there. Later, I learned that I had two apartment mates, and one was to leave in one month, another in a week.

The next morning I looked out my bedroom window and saw the litter exposed by the melting snow: snowmobiles that had ground to a halt in the mud and garbage containers painted with graffiti—not foul words, but gaudy, nonetheless. The view made me think of a scene one might find in the slum district of any big American city. I was grateful for the snow of last evening that had covered much of the trash scattered all over the grounds of the hospital compound.

There were about two-dozen children of all ages romping glee-fully in the playground area between the apartments and the hospital as if they were in a well-groomed park of the towns and cities back East. They were oblivious to the unsightly trash. Later that night, some were still playing at 9:30 or 10:00, evidently grateful for the sunshine of the lengthening days. Most of these children were not Native Alaskans, but were the offspring of parents who were employed in the hospital.

It was my first morning in Bethel, and I began to unpack and make myself at home. I hoped that my boxes, which I had shipped earlier, would arrive soon with my books, lamp, and my personal supply of prescription drugs. They did not arrive for another day or two, which taught me that I should never travel without my pre-scription drugs in my carry-on luggage. The next day, Saturday, I went to the hospital, even though I was not to report to work until Monday. I introduced myself to everyone I saw and solicited help in dealing with the phone system, which I needed to use to let my family know that I had arrived safely. I found that when you talk on a phone with a satellite delay, you tend both to speak while the other party is talking and to shout! It was very frustrating as it sounded as if you were being rude.

The fact that I would not start work until Monday was a blessing, because it gave me time to nose around and talk to the natives and some of the other "tdy" (short for temporary-duty personnel), as they call us when we are on a time-limited assignment.

At the end of day one, I fell sound asleep, renewed by the friendliness of the natives I met in the hospital, who once again affirmed for me that, even in the most dismal surroundings, I could still find beauty in the people and in the work itself. I was disappointed by the barren landscape, dotted with the trash of modern society, but I had come with an open mind, a book of blank pages to fill with my observations of a land that was foreign to me and that, ultimately, would give me a renewed appreciation for the ease of my life back home.

I am intrigued by the value that we place on material comforts, modern gadgets, and high-tech toys in more "civilized" locales. We have so many choices for entertainment, and yet we experience a continual, restless desire for more and more "things." In Bethel, I was grateful for the radio, though I could only get one local station, which featured announcements (frequently in Yupik, the local Native Alaskan language) by inhabitants of all ages and a variety of music that ranged from country to rock to Native Alaskan melodies.

I was also grateful for my laptop computer. I had not taken a printer with me, but, while snooping around in the administrative office, I was delighted to find a printer—an ancient, but working Wang LDP8!!! I would be able to print my letters and whatever else proved necessary.

During my first few days in Bethel, I recorded several interesting comments on my laptop:

- "Two kinds of people come to Alaska; fugitives and prospectors—which are you?"
- When I asked the Emergency Medical Services (EMS) director why he was in Bethel, he replied, "I sobered up one day, and I was in Bethel!" He flies a Medivac plane, which

transports patients from the villages to Bethel when there is an emergency.

- "I am part Eskimo and part Russian, of the Ivanoff family. I was raised in California to get a better education. I have returned to learn the language and lessons of my culture. I am ashamed that I do not know them and I am being taught by my girlfriend, a lovely young Eskimo woman who works as a Community Health Aide (CHA) in the villages."
- "This place will really get to you. It is depressing; the natives are wonderful; you will leave a better nurse. I will be a better physician, but it is a hard place to be for two years. No one stays very long."
- "You will love these people; they are stoic, patient, appreciative, and a pleasure to work with."
- "I am told the natives do not really like the White people. A nurse who implied that a native was stupid was sent home."
- "You will do well here; just be yourself and be friendly with the natives; they will love you!"

This last comment was from Elim, the hospital cafeteria's manager. Elim referred to himself and his employees as "Eskimos" with tongue in cheek. They were actually of the Yupik tribe, as are most of the natives in the Yukon-Kuskokwim delta region. When outsiders refer to them as "Eskimos," they sometimes resent it, unless they have chosen to use the term themselves or have given permission to use it.

Comments on April 25, 1994, my first real day at work:

As with any new job, I spent many hours in orientation. I did see one patient who had an impacted radial fracture. With help, I interpreted the X-ray and with help set her arm with a "sugar-tong splint" that we made ourselves. Already, I was learning how creative one must be in a remote setting that doesn't have the fancy casting equipment and orthopedic devices available back home.

Forty-nine villages in the Delta Region receive healthcare from the Yukon Kuskokwim Delta Regional Hospital in Bethel. The most impressive observation of the day was to listen as a physician communicated with the CHA in each village. The time spent is still called "radio time," recalling the time when these conversations were made across the miles via two-way radios. Now they use the phone.

The aides talk to an assigned doctor every day. I listened to them report the history of a patient's complaint, their physical findings, and the results of certain lab tests they had performed; finally, they report to the doctor their plan of action…. They follow instructions from the doctor and can perform such procedures as starting an intravenous line for fluids or medications, making incisions to drain a boil or abscess, and many of the other tasks that nurse practitioners or physicians' assistants do. They are caring, smart, and most of them have only an eighth grade education plus two years of training by the mid-level practitioners and physicians in Bethel. And they are on call twenty-four hours a day, seven days a week.

In more prosperous areas, nurses will soon be required to have a Bachelor of Science in Nursing. To become a nurse practitioner now, it is suggested and will soon be mandated that one must have a Masters in Nursing. My formal training is quite limited by today's standards. I went to a nursing school—a three-year diploma program in Nashville, Tennessee, from 1954 to 1957. Then there was more emphasis on actual bedside nursing than academics. Nursing was beginning to be a "respectable" profession. The pay was low, and the work was hard. Most of our education actually took place at the bedside, and we were expected to "obey" doctors' orders and keep our opinions to ourselves.

We also had to look good. By that, I mean that our uniforms had to be clean and starched, the hems had to be a certain length, no nail polish or jewelry was permitted, and we always wore our caps with pride. There was never any doubt as to our position. Now it is difficult to know who the players are in a hospital. Everyone wears

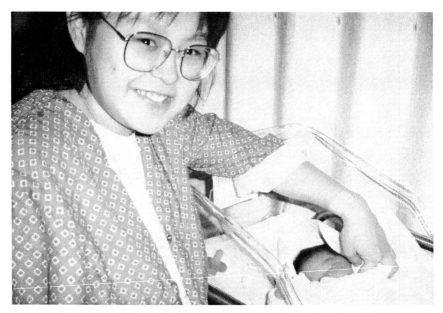

*Aide holding a baby in emergency room at Yukon Kuskokwim
Delta Regional Hospital in Bethel, Alaska (1994).*

"scrubs" and tennis shoes of any color (clean or dirty), and jewelry
and artificial fingernails are allowed. The caps that we used to wear
pinned to the tops of our heads to indicate the school from which
we had graduated were abandoned some time ago and for the most
part, this was for practical reasons, since they did not cover our
hair. To let patients know who is who, nametags are usually manda-
tory. If a patient is alert and can read, he or she will know who you
are. Of course, even after more than twenty-five years, I still get the
question, "What is a nurse practitioner?" If we act like doctors, they
call us doctors. Some think that we are practical nurses, meaning
Licensed Practical Nurses (LPNs). LPNs graduate from a technical
school's two-year nursing program; registered nurses may hold
either a two-year degree (Associate of Science in Nursing) or a
four-year degree (Bachelor of Science in Nursing); nurse practitioners are registered nurses who have special training for advanced
practice, which is usually taken as part of a Masters of Science in
Nursing degree program.

When I returned to North Carolina, nurses were shocked to learn that the CHAs in Alaska could do so many things. This is one of the reasons I call this book *Health Care in the Trenches*. As a nation with the reputation of providing the best (and most expensive) medical care in the world, there are many pockets in this country where the heath care is quite limited. It is in these "trenches" that I have found the caring and compassion that are sometimes missing in the world of high-tech medicine.

My first-hand observation of some of the federally funded hospitals, such as those administered by Indian Health Services, has shown their cost effectiveness to be extremely poor. I have seen the same waste, however, in private hospitals in North Carolina. In Bethel, our patients came from the villages by plane, boat, dog sled, snowmobile, or truck, if the river was frozen. They had no appointments, and we treated them on a first-come-first-served basis. They were charged for visits that were not truly emergencies. In many parts of the United States, there are now some "acute-care" settings (often called "urgent-care centers" or, with tongue in cheek, "Doc in a Box") that charge less, and even in Bethel we had what was called the Fast-Track Clinic. When it was time for a patient to be seen, a mid-level practitioner or a physician could perform triage to determine whether or not to treat the patient as an emergency or in the Fast-Track Clinic, which charges a lower rate. ("Triage" is the medical term that describes the process by which a person in charge quickly evaluates a healthcare situation and then makes a decision as to which patient needs to be seen first and where the person should be seen.)

When I say "charges," I am referring to the bill that is submitted to Indian Health Service, since the natives do not pay for the service. Sometimes a particular hospital or clinic runs out of funds before the fiscal year is over. This is especially problematic if a particular patient needs a procedure such as cataract removal or hip replacement; sometimes a gall bladder removal is delayed because the funds are not available, even though back East, we would think it to be a serious emergency.

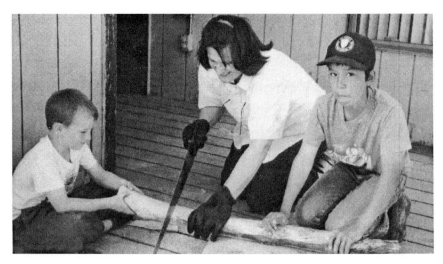

Native children excited over building a birdhouse in Bethel, Alaska (1994).

Having witnessed the inefficient use of time by providers and by patients, the archaic medical-records system, and the limited drug formulary in Bethel, I was amazed that so much was accomplished.

The Native Alaskan patients are stoic, patient, and appreciative, and very soon, I learned the Yupik word for "thank you": "ouyhana."

April 28, 1994, other comments on my first week:

Since I would be working the evening shift, I had the chance to go to town. I donned my winter duds and walked to town in the wet, blowing snow to open an account at a local bank, go by the post office, and check out the local store. Yes, there is only one store. It is called the "AC," short for "Alaska Commercial," a general store, selling groceries, hardware, clothes, crafts, and various other things. It is clean and quite well stocked.

The hospital cafeteria had provided meal tickets for my first few days, but I was almost out of them, so I needed to think about cooking, although I had avoided the apartment kitchen so far. So I picked up a few items—beans, rice, spaghetti, spaghetti sauce and post cards. These few items, which would have cost about seven dollars back home, came to more than thirteen dollars!

Since I needed to get back in time to go to work, I took a taxi. There are only thirteen miles of paved road and eighteen miles of unpaved roads in Bethel, but there are at least five taxi companies and about twenty taxis! For two dollars, you can take a taxi to any place in town. While this sounds like a bargain, you need to remember that the taxi drivers put as many people in one taxi as it will hold.

I wanted to write about all of the patients I saw. Instead, I will limit myself to a few cases that I hope will trigger your imagination. First, let me clarify that all of my patients in this setting were of the Yupik Tribe of Native Alaskans. Occasionally, I did see a native Athabascan and more rarely, a non-native who was an employee of the hospital or the town:

- A ten-year-old boy had been vomiting and had a fever. When I asked what he had last eaten, he said, "Caribou stew." I was a little startled: in all of my years of nursing, this was the first time I had heard that response. However, the child had strep throat, so his presentation was really no different from kids back in North Carolina.

- A six-month-old boy with bronchiolitis had an X-ray that was read as "atelecstasis and markings of chronic disease." How could an infant already have markings of "chronic" disease? However, many of the children in the Yukon have respiratory problems. On any given day, I would see at least one mother with an infant prone across her lap while she pounded the baby's back with cupped hands to loosen up the phlegm and congestion. (This was not the type of Native American drumming that I had anticipated.) This drumming was a technique I had learned as a student nurse in the '50s when I worked in a tuberculosis (TB) hospital. For this kind of ailment, we treated most of the kids and some adults with a shot of Rocephin, an antibiotic that needs to be administered in two doses separated by twelve hours. In this case, mom wanted her infant to be admitted to the hospital for treatment because she had come from one of the villages

9

many miles away. The physician explained to her that hospitalization was not appropriate. (Doesn't that sound just like the president of a Health Maintenance Organization?)

- A social worker came to see the mother, and together they found a place for her to spend the night in Bethel. It seems that everyone in the Delta region is related, so the families always make room for one or two more, if necessary. The child received his Rocephin injection and a breathing treatment, and by the next morning, he was indeed improved—the treatment was repeated, and they flew back to their village. (Indian Health issues each patient who is flown into Bethel a "coupon," worth about two hundred dollars, for a round-trip flight.)

Because so many of the patients had to travel long distances to reach the medical facilities in Bethel, it was also imperative and prudent that I address not only each patient's current complaint or symptoms, but also that I scrutinize the chart and determine what other medical needs he or she might need for us to attended to in order to avoid another costly trip in the near future. For example, a man I saw with a case of cellulitis also had active tuberculosis and needed a repeat chest X-ray while he was in Bethel. Another case involved a woman I saw for removal of a deeply set splinter who also wanted a pregnancy test—which came back positive. She also was an alcoholic. So before she returned home, she was referred to the Obstetric Clinic, had a pap smear and some lab work, started her prenatal vitamins, and was referred to the Celebration of Life program. The Celebration of Life program is designed to use strengths of cultural traditions in the Delta to provide a "Circle of Care" around pregnant women who wish to remain substance-free during and after pregnancy. I learned about this federally funded program at grand rounds.

"Grand rounds" is another old-fashioned term. In a teaching hospital, young physicians in training follow teaching physicians around the hospital to see a certain number of patients as a learning experience. The meaning of the term has expanded to include the regular staff meetings that caregivers attend to learn about a variety of cases and how each was managed or mismanaged in order to improve the facility's overall quality of care. Most hospitals still refer to these meetings as "grand rounds." Every provider is expected to go to "rounds" each Wednesday, whether or not they are on duty. I have to admit that the case studies presented there each week were fascinating and very educational. I learned about gunshot wounds, smoke inhalation, and one man who had rectal cancer and committed suicide after he had been diagnosed and treated. I also learned about severe congestive heart failure complicated by chronic asthma.

Another common illness in the Delta is mastoiditis, which usually requires surgical intervention. This is not quite the common ear infection with which I and other American healthcare providers are so well acquainted. This disease involves the mastoid area behind the ear, which becomes infected when a common ear infection is not discovered and treated in a timely way. When a Yupik mom says her child has pus coming from the ear, you can believe that it is truly a foul, copious, yellow exudate and not just the excessive wax that we often see back home. Coincidentally, my own father had a hearing loss in one ear for that very reason. He had developed a severe ear infection with subsequent mastoiditis and had had surgery to correct the problem. I thought the condition no longer occurred, but working in Bethel showed me that assumption was incorrect.

As for the social life of a "tdy" employee: Over the years, I have made friends with patients and co-workers alike. In Bethel, my co-workers became my extended family. Ann, an obstetric nurse from Georgia, was about my age and had an even larger sense of adventure than I had. She had been working in Bethel for more than six years, which was almost a record. She was funny and wise, and I knew we would be good friends.

Going into town requires that you walk on the boardwalk because the surrounding, half-thawed tundra lets you sink into the earth if you don't. This is why there are so few miles of paved road. Ever since the U.S. Army Air Corp was here in World War II, attempts to build runways and roadways have been thwarted by the ever-shifting soft earth.

Ann and I walked into town on the boardwalk in the rain with our backpacks like schoolgirls. We may not have looked as young as schoolgirls, but we had the enthusiasm and energy of youth from the experience of our lives. We stopped at the AC (the general store), and went into Gloria's Coffee Shop (not to be confused with the fancy Gloria Jean's Coffee Shops in many locations of the lower forty-eight). It seemed to be a popular gathering place for the locals. As we prepared to leave, I wanted to go to the restroom before walking back to the compound. Ann had a mischievous smile on her face as she offered to get the key.

With that, she went to the proprietor and returned with a key attached via a half-inch chain about two feet long and attached to a shovel handle. I got the giggles. Of course, I had the attention of every native as I walked out with my key. There was evidence of polite amusement on their faces at this "gussik," the name the natives give to non-natives, probably derived from Cossack, the Russians who were the first non-natives who came to Alaska. I think the owners of this establishment were serious about keeping up with the restroom keys.

Ann showed me all around the town. The buildings are run down. Every scrap of wood is treasured for any type of construction. There was only one tree. The natives retrieve the wood from the mountains when the Kuskokwim River breaks in the spring, bringing trees and parts of wrecked boats rushing toward the Bering Sea. It truly looks like a town of great poverty. The Baptist Church is in a Quonset hut. In fact, the first hospital in town was in a Quonset hut that is still standing. The interior was in ruins, but the rusty metal building survived. Some people were living in metal train cars that had come to Bethel up the river with a load of supplies and had been commandeered by an enterprising individual. I was astounded.

More Observations

April 30, 1994

On the wall of the clinic this sign was posted:

> *"Let us tighten our bond as a knot would*
> *and unite love's great power*
> *To redirect the present condition*
> *we are facing in our lives."*

Everywhere I looked there were platitudes, words of wisdom and encouragement. The words were for all of us—the gussicks and the natives—and were meant to improve our present conditions and challenge us to hold on to a value system that will improve the length and quality of our lives.

My shift—12:00 noon to 10:00 p.m.—was very busy. Some of the patients had been waiting all morning. Once they have made the trip to Bethel from the villages, it was imperative that you ask about any problems or needs, besides the current complaint, that should be addressed. For example:

- A forty-one-year-old-man was seen because he fell on slippery steps the day before, sustaining an ankle injury. I asked if there were any other injuries. He answered, "No." I asked him to remove his dark glasses and saw that he had the worst black eye I had ever seen. Besides the purple, blue, and green discoloration, there was a hard collection of blood over his cheek that felt like a tumor and was actually a firm hematoma. I was also concerned about the appearance of the pupil in his injured eye until I realized that he had had a cataract removed and a lens implant. I was surprised at this finding, given his relatively young age. The truth was that he had other injuries from previous falls, and, yes, each time he had been drinking alcohol, another problem commonly seen in Bethel. (For that matter, alcohol-related problems are common in most of the acute care settings I have worked in across the country. There were more seen at the University of Massachusetts during fraternities' and sororities' "rush" week than at Indian Health Services!)

- During one shift, the variety of complaints was extensive. On a particular evening, I saw three children less than five years old who were examined for infections and really had to be evaluated for sexual abuse. In every place where I have worked, the stated reason for coming to the doctor is often not always the real reason for coming. In a patient's history, we state "CC"—for chief complaint—and we should add "ARC" to indicate the patient's "actual reason for coming."

- A seventy-year-old man had a fractured skull and had sustained a ruptured eardrum. The bleeding had filled up the scalp and the left side of his face, yet he was coherent and even laughing. He was air lifted to Anchorage for some high-tech care.

- I saw the worst cases of scabies with secondary infection in my career, worse even than I had seen in a textbook. It turned out that the patient's family's village had had a major epidemic. In two cases, I sent home enough medicine to treat eleven family or household members.

- I also saw a four-hundred-pound, thirty-two-year-old woman who had cellulitis secondary to a stasis ulcer of her left leg. The ulcer had been wrapped with an unna boot (an occlusive dressing meant to aid in the healing of the infection) just that morning. It was so uncomfortable that she had ripped it off and returned and was admitted to the hospital. When I finally came home about 11:00 p.m., some of the best nurses, Emergency Medical Technicians (EMTs), and lab technicians had made eight attempts to draw her blood from her elusive veins and start an IV.

- Among others seen that day were several who had either newly diagnosed or old cases of tuberculosis. Almost all of the natives who were more than fifty years old had been infected with tuberculosis at some time in their lives. Not only was there evidence of lung infections with old scars, but there were also cases of tuberculosis of the bones and kidneys.

At Grand Rounds one day, we were told the story of a female physician, "Dr. Mike." The story goes that in the early '50s, INH and Streptomycin had been discovered to treat tuberculosis. In the Delta region, the disease was rampant. Dr. Mike was sent to Bethel with enough medicine to treat the residents of the area. People were getting well. She was typing her reports to send back to Washington with the results of her success and to request more drugs. Questions came to her about her need for more drugs. It turned out that natives from other villages were coming in by dog sled or walking to get the INH and Streptomycin for their families. The health officials told Dr. Mike that she was to only treat those folks in Bethel. She stopped typing her reports, and they began sending her whatever quantity she requested. (I suppose that is why we all have such terrible handwriting!) When the officials from Washington made their next visit to the Delta region, they were astounded that so many people had been cured of tuberculosis. When they learned of Dr. Mike's deception, she was discharged from her duties and went home to Minnesota because she had not followed orders. What irony and stupidity, in my opinion. As I sat in the meeting hearing this story that sounded like ancient history, I realized that these drugs had been discovered at the same time I was in nursing school.

My Aunt Lelia had tuberculosis of the kidney in 1956, and I would go to her house twice a week to give her Streptomycin injections. Boy, did I feel old!

Later, I heard the sirens and a physician asking a nurse, "Are they coming in or going out?" "Going out where?" she asked. Her answer was, "To the river." Two men had fallen through the ice on the Kuskokwim where it was beginning to thaw. The predicted "break up" of the river was May 15. People place wagers on the minute and hour the river will break. They somehow submerge a clock through the water in the fall and the exact time of the break is recorded. In 1994, the pot was $5000. I had arrived in Bethel too late to place a bet.

The Yupik are very intelligent, and when we teach them about their illnesses and plans of care, they ask good questions. My concerns revolve around what I see as paternalistic care, rather than care that empowers them to take more responsibility for their health and make good choices in their lifestyles. This is not a new song for me to sing. For years, I have preached about *rights*: rights to health care, rights to an improved economic status, rights to better lives that can only be achieved if the recipients take on some responsibility. This is true for the affluent, as well as for those less fortunate. My experience in Bethel simply confirmed my belief.

Let me comment on my living conditions. I lived in a three-bedroom apartment at the hospital compound. During the time I was there, people came and left, sometimes leaving clothes and personal belongings behind. One female employee was to visit with her husband for five days in Anchorage. He had driven up from Texas, and when he got to Seattle, had chest pain and learned that he needed emergency bypass surgery. Of course, she did not return to Bethel. A couple of her new friends came later to pack up her clothes and send them to her.

I never knew who was moving in next. A woman who was a laboratory technician from Michigan moved in after a few weeks, and we became friends. I will call her Anastasia. She chose that name for herself. She was really free-spirited, with lots of ambition for living in the wild woods of Michigan. She had personally built her own house, heated by wood she cut herself, and there was still no plumbing in the place. She had an undaunted spirit and saw beauty in a bird or bush on the tundra that many of us would have missed. She gathered enough scrap wood to build a birdhouse, which fascinated some of our neighbor children. As I mentioned, wood is a rare commodity in Bethel. Since there are only a few trees in that part of the wilderness, there is a race to gather the wood that floats down the river once the ice breaks. Natives and gussicks, alike, take to their boats or clamber along the riverside to retrieve logs, old lumber, or flats that have fallen from barges during the previous year. Many dwellings are primitive, having been made from any scrap of building material that can be found. I have never witnessed anything like this.

News travels fast. We learned that the "ivory man" was arriving from Nome. Only the Native Alaskans are allowed to carve objects from walrus ivory. A master carver who lived in Nome came to Bethel twice a year. He brought objects to sell that he had carved in

The "Ivory Man" from Nome, Alaska showing his wares in Bethel, Alaska (1994).

ivory and other natural materials. He would set up shop in a private home, and everyone who was interested in his wares would go there. I could not resist buying two necklaces, one for my sister, Joy, and one for myself. I would have loved to buy several intricate carvings of polar bears, birds of the tundra, and even depictions of a village with Native Alaskan figures and igloos. The expense was an issue, not to mention the task of getting anything back home, so I did not succumb to temptation. Now I regret that I did not buy more.

From my journal: "It is May now, and May in Bethel is unfamiliar to me. From back home, I hear that my family is preparing to open the swimming pool and having picnics and cookouts. I went to a couple of salmon cookouts here and wore my winter duds, which felt wonderful. In North Carolina, the trees and flowers have probably exploded with color and everything is covered with pollen. One thing that I do not miss in Bethel is the pollen."

More patient stories:

- A young woman came in with a breast abscess the size of a teacup. I was hoping that one of the three doctors I was working with would perform the necessary incision and drainage. However, I was told that I needed the "experience." Fortunately, I was successful in draining the abscess and inserting a wick. I thought of my daughter, Becky, who had a breast hematoma following the removal of a cyst. The procedure was so painful because a knife was used to penetrate the breast (without anesthesia) so the pooled blood could come out. You can imagine that I felt the pain that I had to inflict upon this patient as much as she did. She cried, and I almost cried with her.

- Reading X-rays was a new experience for me. The doctors, other mid-level providers, and the radiologist were all helpful. (To my colleagues who disdain the term "mid-level": I apologize to your sensitive natures—the reality is that we are categorized as such in most of the country, and it is not always considered an insult!) We ordered many chest films, and I was intrigued that the status of a lung infection could change over a twenty-four-hour period.

- Tobacco is a way of life in Bethel. Not only do they smoke cigarettes, but they also dip and chew tobacco. I have seen parents put a bit of tobacco in a child's mouth to soothe him. The dentists are very busy treating dental caries (cavities) from prolonged bottle-feeding and from the effects of the tobacco.

- A precious seven-year-old girl named Tiana was sleeping when I went into the exam room to see her. Her mother woke her up and began to tell me the story of the young girl's symptoms. She complained of a headache, could no longer write on the lines of her school papers, and had experienced changes in her vision. When I had her follow my finger with her eyes, they did not track appropriately, and the fundoscopic examination revealed some pappiledema (swelling of the optic nerve). While we were talking, she was singing, "I am special, I am me," reminding me of my own sweet, singing grandchildren. As I examined her, she could not focus on my fingers. Her eyes danced the typical dance of nystagmus. She could not walk heel-to-toe. I suspected a brain tumor. The physician who was working with me that day agreed. The little girl was sent to Anchorage for a neurological evaluation. Most of the time when a referral is needed, it takes days, weeks, or even longer to get an appointment. Thankfully, she was sent the next day. From there, she was sent to Providence Children's Hospital in Seattle, Washington, where the tumor was successfully removed in June, before I completed this assignment, Sometimes, I never see the patients again. I had the opportunity to see Tiana once more. After her surgery in Seattle, she had been admitted to the hospital in Bethel because of a crisis with her medication. The tumor had been attached to her pituitary gland, and she now needed small doses of pituitary hormone, to be administered daily by her mother. The nurses had pre-filled the syringes with the colorless medication. Evidently, one of the syringes her mother had used had had no medication in it, and without her medication, Tiana was in deep trouble. After she was admitted to the hospital in Bethel, I began visiting her daily. I took a young pediatric resident with me to meet her and hear her story. When I asked if she remembered me, she replied, "Yes, you are the funny one who showed me the magic coloring book." I asked her to sing her sweet song for the pediatrician. She sang, "I am happy, I am me. I have two eyes, I can see," and before she could finish the song, my own eyes welled with tears: because of the operation to remove the tumor, Tiana could no longer see. She was blind. A friend of mine, a nurse practitioner named Joyce, had given me a lovely hand-woven Vietnamese bag. Joyce had worked with many of the mountain folk of Vietnam who had come to

Tiana, age seven, recovering from removal of a brain tumor, Bethel Alaska (1994).

North Carolina to settle. It was woven of many colors and with many different stitches. Joyce had asked me to give this to someone in Alaska. I decided that Tiana would receive this gift. I told her the story of where it was made. I took her fingers and had her trace the different stitches and know the colors of each stitch. I told her that the colors represented people from another land and of another culture. I suggested that each time she ran her fingers over the stitches, she should think of all the people in the world and know that she was loved. At this time, Tiana was alive and well. Her family still believed that she would see again. They know now that this will not happen. Yet she will perceive things that you or I or other sighted people may never see. What a privilege for me to have met Tiana.

- A seventy-two-year-old Yupik gentleman had flown in with a Community Health Aide from his village. It was a forty-five-minute trip, and the CHA had held the patient's nose all the way as he was having a horrendous nose bleed. The doctor in the emergency room taught me how to use a nasal catheter to pack his nose. I cannot tell you enough about the value of the Community Health Aides in Indian Health. They are bright and caring. I have learned a great deal about commitment and compassion from these people.

Everyone here has a story. Everyone has come to Alaska for a reason. There are no native gussicks. We are all immigrants, so to speak, from the "lower forty-eight" as the natives say. To write their stories would be another book in itself. As we Americans move about in this great country for whatever reason, we are all more nomadic than we may realize. It would be interesting to do a study on how many Americans are nomads, compared to those who are born, educated, and remain in their hometown or state for a lifetime. I have no answers here, only questions.

Days off:

What does "day off" in Bethel mean? For me, it meant doing a little laundry, a little housekeeping, taking a walk to town for dinner at the "Snack Shack," correspondence, and writing. In early May, when I woke at 6:15 a.m., the temperature was thirty-one degrees, and it was snowing. The cold wind was biting, and I realized that winter on the tundra must be hard. I was glad to be here in May. I ordered only halibut at the restaurants because Ann, my nurse friend, told me never to buy salmon at a restaurant or store; salmon fishing would begin in a few weeks, and then you could buy it fresh and clean and cook it yourself. I really needed a filet knife. Imagine how startled I was to see a native drag a sixty-pound salmon up on the porch and start cutting it up.

By now, I was getting mail from home almost daily. It warmed my chilled body, as well as my heart. Despite the lengthening days, I learned to sleep in daylight. Many people have blackout shades or aluminum foil on their bedroom windows to keep the light out.

There are pharmacists who work here from the U. S. Public Health Service. There are only a few who work here full time. The others come on temporary assignment and travel to other areas as well. One pharmacist who had been to Bethel a number of times taught me some interesting things about the area. He had recently returned from an Indian Health Hospital in Santa Fe, New Mexico. The natives there appreciated a raucous sort of humor, much like my many of my friends in North Carolina and Tennessee. When he came here he noticed that the Yupik are very soft spoken and were intimidated by his loud, joking style. He was told that the Yupik call gussicks "children of thunder," meaning that we are too loud in our speech and a little wild in our gestures. My lesson for that day was to speak more softly and respectfully to these gentle people.

While on the subject of pharmacy, I want to comment on the "formulary." Having worked for so many years in health care's private sector, my prescribing habits allowed me to write many different prescriptions, as long as they were appropriate and included in the patient-care guidelines. In Indian Health and in the Veteran's Administration healthcare system, the list of allowed prescriptions is quite limited. I had trouble with this for some time. Since I returned to North Carolina, however, I find that I am more cautious and prudent in my prescribing. I have learned that the older tried-and-true drugs do work and are less expensive and in many situations, less risky. And there is more attention being paid by insurers and Health Maintenance Organizations to limit the prescriptions that may be filled.

Alaska Stories Continued

More emergency room experiences:

- A four-year-old boy had a nasty splinter in his thigh. I needed to make a one-half-inch incision in his thigh to get it out. I was thankful for TAC, a topical anesthetic that is worth its weight in gold. With TAC on his skin and a little distraction with my magic sticks I pulled out of my pocket, he did not feel the lidocaine injection or the incision.

Once again I learned that conservative treatment is not always the best plan for these folks. They seem to have compromised immune systems, and I have seen about four patients with "normal" chest films to whom I did not give antibiotics. They were back in two days with lung infiltrates and high fevers. If they live in one of the villages, that means two plane trips to Bethel. I should have learned better by now.

- The local police pick up anyone who is intoxicated. They bring them to the emergency room for medical clearance, meaning we have to determine if the patient is truly intoxicated or if there is a medical problem that needs to be addressed. If they are in no immediate medical crisis, they go to jail for protective custody. Since this a dry town, they drink anything. In one case the "beverage" was Listerine. The exam room reeked of mouthwash instead of alcohol. Except for the patient's lacerated forehead and obvious intoxication, one may have thought it was rather antiseptic.

An older gentleman was sitting in a wheel chair waiting for me to give him medical clearance after being picked up by the police. Many of the natives over fifty years of age still speak Yupik more than English, and I was informed that he might not understand my questions. I introduced myself, as I always do, and proceeded to listen to his heart. He looked up at me with his rheumy eyes and said, "Do you know how to *!\#? When I said, "I beg your pardon," he made a vulgar gesture that means the same in every language. I simply said, "No," and proceeded with my examination.

Comments on my "social" life in Bethel:

I came home one evening and was surprised to see that the room across the hall had its door shut. Then I heard a cough. I went to bed, to be awakened the next morning by the doorbell. A man named Tom was looking for Wendy. I could only assume that I had a new apartment mate and that it was not a serial killer or a homeless person who had made his or her way into the apartment across the hall. Wendy and Tom were medical residents from Minnesota who had arrived the night before. I sensed their first impressions were very much like mine and found myself to be the welcoming committee with words of encouragement, as if I were not a short-timer myself.

The next day was relatively quiet except that there seemed to be too many providers, medical students, residents, doctors, and actually fewer patients than usual. Part of the reason for the low turnout was related to the approaching time for the Kuskokwim River's ice to break. The natives and "old timers" said that the river had not had a dramatic break in about five years. With less-dramatic spring warming, the river had melted more gradually, and as the waters flowed under the ice with the tides of the Kuskokwim Bay, the Bering Sea, and the Pacific Ocean, there was no spectacular show for us to see in 1994.

On the day before, however, you could hear, for the first time, a sound like tinkling glass along with the rush of the river. The sound reminded me of wind chimes or of ice cubes being shaken gently in a glass. I went to the river in the morning, and it was now still and silent; the ice had a mosaic pattern, and small rivulets of water surrounded some of those patterns. By eight o'clock, when I returned, the entire scene was not only moving, but it also picked up speed as we watched. By 8:30, it suddenly stopped. Was the tide changing? No, there was a jam "up-river." The jam consisted of large chunks of ice, logs, and other debris. A jam demands respect. Jams back-up the river, causing it to overflow, and there can be serious flooding. Everyone went down to the river to watch as it rose closer and closer to the land's edge in town.

Three days later, on May 14, at 3:30 p.m., the river actually broke. Two winners shared the $5000 prize money. I had returned to take pictures in the sunlight that morning, and everything was still under the ice crystals, though it had begun to find its way downstream, and once again, the ice crystals made their magical music. The impact this event made on the community was remarkable. There was a flurry of activity because the natives knew that as soon as the river began to flow again, their lives would change. The patients felt an urgent need, described to me as "river-break fever," to have their medical problems attended to before they started fishing. As soon as it became possible, the natives put their boats in the water and began netting salmon and other fish. The "fish camps" along the river began to open, and the activity that is one of their only means of livelihood was underway until next winter, when the river would freeze once again.

Setting up fish camps is an important part of life on the Kuskokwim River. A fish camp in Alaska is quite different from those in the lower forty-eight and especially from those in Tennessee where I grew up. Each native family claims a portion of land on the river. Here they establish sleeping quarters, using either tents or other primitive shelters made from a variety of building

"Fish camp" on Kuskokwim River, Alaska (1994).

materials. The women stay in the camps and keep the fires going while the men are fishing all summer. The women are skilled at putting the cleaned fish on racks for drying in the sun or hanging in their primitive smokehouses. They eat, sleep, play, and work fishing, since their catch will be their sustenance for the long winter ahead. There are certain hours each day when the natives are the only ones who can fish for subsistence. Others are not allowed to fish during these times.

Before returning to the lower forty-eight, I had the opportunity to ride in a wooden boat up the river to a camp where an Athabascan woman served us a piece of freshly smoked salmon. I must say that I have tasted none so good since.

The mother of a fisherman was tending the camp. After the fish were cleaned, she would hang them on racks to dry. In a roughly made smokehouse (not unlike our old tobacco-drying houses in the South), the salmon were hung over alder-wood fires that provided a distinctive smoky flavor to this fish. When I buy this food at the grocery or specialty stores, it does not taste the same as the fish I sampled that day. It was more tender and delicious. There were two children with her who had a makeshift playground, a rubber tire hanging from a tree, and they helped, to some extent, with the fish. A fire was kept going at all times, not only for warmth, but also for cooking their meals. Can you imagine spending your summer in this fashion? They seemed happy with their situation and with our company.

On May 15, Ann and I flew to a village called Quinhagak at the mouth of the Kuskokwim River near the Bering Sea to evaluate the possible medical needs of some of the inhabitants. Quinhagak is typical of the villages on the tundra. As we flew in on the small plane, we saw rows of government houses. These houses have the potential of being comfortable and charming, even neat. It reminded me of a monopoly board. The houses are on stilts in preparation for installing septic systems and running water like we had in Bethel. At this time none of this had been done in this village. Sanitation is a major problem. They must haul all their water, and

Home visit with a Yupik couple in Quinhagak, Alaska (1994)

in each bathroom, in place of a commode, is the "honey bucket," a large plastic bucket with a plastic liner with chemicals in it. There is a collection program for the honey buckets, but many times the waste is simply dumped on the tundra.

As we entered the first house, I learned first hand about cultural diversity. The smell of freshly killed game was overwhelming. The dead carcasses of geese were lying out on a table in the anteroom with pools of blood that had dried as it had dripped from the wounds. This reminded me of Renaissance oil paintings in art museums that portray the freshly killed rabbits or other game lying with fruit, vegetables, and bouquets of flowers on richly carved wooden tables. When I inquired about the health risks of such a practice, our interpreter suggested that we not ask. For hundreds of years the natives have survived by hunting, fishing, and preserving the game as they always have, and their customs are to be respected.

Of course, the small houses are filled with all of their worldly possessions; clothes are piled everywhere. As you know, winter clothing, as well as fishing and hunting equipment, all take a lot of space. There were lots of photographs on the walls of beautiful family members; there were televisions sets (yes, they receive satellite TV, and *Oprah* is one of the Yupiks' favorite programs), telephones (whether they worked or not), pots and pans, etc. Some houses had organized clutter. Others made it difficult for us to get around or find a place to sit. Many people in the lower forty-eight save every string, every newspaper, and fill their homes with unnecessary items. In Alaska, where isolation is a way of life, I could see why every item was kept in easy reach. I also noted that, in every home that we visited, there were coffee cans for spitting tobacco. Everyone seems to use snuff and chew as well as smoke. One lady was very offended when we asked about her smoking habits. Even the children are given snuff at age two or three, and the dentists in Bethel stay busy working on bottle and tobacco caries. Again, this had been a way of life for them for at least a century.

The weather is very hard on the houses and buildings. The wind blows even when the weather is good; the paint really takes a beating, and one might as well forget about clean windows. Most houses have only one door, and all I could think was "fire hazard."

In every yard there is also a great deal of what you might call clutter. Again, wood in a treeless environment is precious, so any wood pallets, boards, or logs pulled out of the river are stashed everywhere. They heat with both wood and oil (often whale oil) stoves, which smoke a great deal and explains the dark stains of their hands, feet, and faces. It is not that they do not wash; it's that the air in the closed houses and steam houses simply leave their mark. For their personal hygiene, most use the steam houses, which are built separate from the dwellings. I have seen some pretty bad burns from getting too close to the fires. Their phrase for this practice is "taking the steam," and their history points to the spiritual aspects of this practice.

Just as in the lower forty-eight, some of the people were more friendly and warm than others. Some were a little skeptical about our visit. Some professed to not speak English until we were ready to leave, and they understood that we were there to help them in a number of ways. We were really doing a needs assessment. There were those with mischief and humor in their conversation. My favorite visit was to the home of an elderly couple who were friendly, kept their home quite tidy, and were very talkative. As we prepared to leave, the gentleman quoted Scripture to me in English! He said that the Bible tells us to love everyone of all races. I challenged him with gentle humor, asking if that also included gussicks. He laughed and that wonderful face with its toothless smile and twinkling eyes endeared him to me. I taught him and his wife to say "I love you" in American Sign Language and even with hands twisted and gnarled in arthritic deformities, they were able to sign the same to me.

My only near disaster that day was my use of the honey bucket. It was no problem to sit on and use, but I have a habit of leaning to one side to clean myself, and in doing so, I almost turned the honey bucket over. I knew that such an event would wear out my welcome in a big way. Fortunately I recovered my balance, and there were no major catastrophes to explain.

More Alaska Stories

Here are some more stories about patients I saw in Bethel:

- A twenty-nine-month-old child was brought in by his mother. The child was screaming intermittently and literally writhing in pain. He had been seen the evening before for what was thought to be a viral gastroenteritis. I suspected that the child was suffering from intussusception, where the bowel loops over itself. It can be a life-threatening illness. Because the radiologist did not think my diagnosis was valid, he was not happy about giving this child the barium enema that I ordered. I elicited the support of the physician working with me. The barium enema was done. Many times this alone will correct the problem. In this case, the intussusception was not totally corrected by the enema, and the child was sent to the Indian Hospital in Anchorage for further care.

I have some opinions about the amount of time it took from the time of admission to diagnosis, but I had come to understand the term "tundra time." It means that no one, absolutely no one, seems to be in a hurry around here. They sleep late, go to school late, and arrive for their appointments late; it is an accepted custom.

- One evening, we had what is known as a "Code Yellow." There had been a fire in a house in Kotlick, one of the villages. Four adults and three children were brought in by Medivac for treatment of burns and inhalation injuries. This was the first and only time while I was in Bethel that I witnessed folks preparing and going into action efficiently. Everything was done well, and only one infant and the mother had to be flown to Anchorage for further treatment. I may have been too hasty to say that everything takes place on tundra time.

- I saw a forty-two-year-old man who suffered seizures due to alcohol withdrawal. He had three seizures in a row, and after aggressive treatment with seizure medicine and electrolytes, he was admitted for further observation. My tendency is to try to help the patent understand the effects that alcohol has on the body and to give tender, loving care. The physicians were more realistic and knew that he had been seen by a substance-abuse counselor for seven to eight years and would probably be seen again and again.

- I also saw a rape victim who refused to be examined by a male. It was the first time that I had gone through all the steps for a rape case, and it took almost three hours. After I returned to work in North Carolina, I learned that nurses specially trained to do this are on call and will come in to perform all of the necessary examinations and tests, as well as collect the many items of evidence, from pubic hair to articles of clothing, etc. This is really a time-saver for the emergency-room physicians.

- A middle-aged man who spoke only Yupik crushed an index finger, breaking a bone in his fingertip. A deep laceration had left the tip of his finger barely dangling. I really wanted the doctor to do this repair but, as usual, they encouraged me to carry on. Fortunately, a native male Community Health Aide was there and taught me to use two liters of normal saline to cleanse the finger before I did anything else. It was his experience that if a wound was cleansed adequately, the repair has a ninety-percent chance of healing. After I anesthetized the finger with a local numbing agent,

I put the finger back in place with three loose sutures. It was with great difficulty that I pushed the needle through the tough fingernail. The man just kept smiling. I never dreamed that he would have a successful recovery. I prescribed antibiotics, had him stay in Bethel for a week, and saw him every day. My repair worked!

- On the last day of my work, two young women were brought in on stretchers. They appeared to be sleeping. After further evaluation, it was apparent that their muscles had just totally relaxed, most evident in the fact that their pupils were dilated, even when we shined a light into their eyes. This muscular paralysis is caused by botulism. When the muscles begin to shut down, the eventual death of the heart muscle will cause death in an untreated patient.

The elders in their community had dug up whitefish buried months before. After a while, the fish rots and is appropriately called "stinkfish." It is considered a delicacy. The older generation has evidently developed immunity to this potentially deadly organism. These young women wanted to taste this fish for the first time. As a result, they had botulism. Fortunately, there is an antidote, and after treatment, they recovered. A young resident from Johns Hopkins was assigned to this case, along with the permanent physicians. I doubt that he will ever see such a case again. I certainly do not expect to.

The bacterium B. Botulinus, which causes botulism, produces a deadly toxin, yet the medical profession, especially plastic surgeons, use Botox, a derivative of that toxin, to inject into wrinkles, causing them to relax and giving patients a youthful and sometimes surprised look to their faces. Now people have Botox "parties," much like Tupperware parties, where the invitees can all have the injections at one time. The bad news is that Botox's effect only lasts about six months, but for about $100 a shot, the injection can be repeated regularly.

On July 1, I had the opportunity to fly with the bush pilots and an Emergency Medical Technician to a village where some violence had resulted in injuries. I quickly packed all of my emergency rations, sleeping bag, etc, and rushed over to the hospital. Each of us was expected to carry a fifty-pound backpack with emergency supplies. Despite the date, it was cold. We flew over the tundra at 2:00 a.m., and I was astounded by the view. On the tundra there were hundreds of silvery ponds, still frozen. Of course, the land appeared to be flat. I could see both the sun and the moon, as well as streaks of silver-lined clouds on the horizon. When we got to the village, we had to go to the river and get in an old wooden boat. The banks of the river were muddy because of the thaw, and with the extra weight we carried, we stepped into what seemed like quicksand. Fortunately, the "highway patrol" (this term amuses me because there are no highways!) had also flown in their plane, since the reported injury was caused by violence—in this case, a fight between two men. The officers helped us to get on board the craft. The boat was primitive, but they offered me an old Formica-covered kitchen chair, probably because I was the oldest on board. The Yupik native who piloted the boat was skilled, and as we sped down the Yukon River, I was exhilarated, but really cold!

Finally we arrived at a landing near the village. We hauled our gear out of the boat, sinking a bit in the soft tundra beach of the river. We walked for almost a mile to the clinic. Everyone in town was there. The patient had been drinking, as had been his assailant, who happened to be his brother-in-law! There had been an argument over the victim's sister, and the brother-in-law had slashed open the patient's abdomen with a knife. There were three CHAs in this clinic, and they had done a marvelous job of stabilizing the patient—an IV had been established, a cardiac monitor was in place, and his heart was stable. They had applied wet abdominal packs to his wound and reinforced them to hold in his intestines. The law officers finished their investigation and left. After the EMT had completed her assessment, we had to get the patient back to the boat and from there to the plane that would transport him to the hospital in Bethel. A wound of this nature is called an evisceration, since the intestines were exposed. Of course we were concerned about the patient's blood loss and knew that he would need an expert surgeon. Once we got him to Bethel, he would have to fly Medivac (a medical-transport plane equipped like an intensive care unit) to Anchorage.

With the help of two natives, we carried the stretcher on the boardwalk a long distance. I have to be honest: as we walked in the moonlight, with the sky so bright and the cotton flowers swaying in the wind, I realized that, at fifty-nine years of age, carrying the patient's IV bag, I was thrilled at being part of his rescue. We walked for a long time, longer than it had taken us to walk from the boat. The people carrying the stretcher could not all fit on the boardwalk, and we needed to set the stretcher down periodically so they could change places. I was worried about how we could get the stretcher into the boat without dumping him in the river. Then I realized that we were walking all the way back to the Twin Otter airplane. Once we were established on the plane, it was just a matter of monitoring his vital signs and his wound until we arrived in Bethel. I learned that these natives cannot stand for their feet to stay under a blanket. We kept covering up his cold feet, and he kept kicking the covers off. We were afraid of possible excessive blood loss and possible shock. Once we arrived in Bethel, the ambulance transported us to the hospital. The staff was ready for us, despite the fact that three motor-vehicle-accident patients were being cared for at the same time. New intravenous lines were established, dressings were changed, a Foley catheter inserted (we did not know if his bladder had been cut), and of course, antibiotics, pain medicines, and other medications were started. Within an hour he was on his way to the native hospital in Anchorage. We later learned that he had suffered only a small laceration of his intestines. The repair went well, and he was to come back to Bethel in a few days. Needless to say, it was a memorable night for this aging nurse practitioner.

Carl came to visit me in Bethel in May. Although I had described my first impressions of Bethel to him, he seemed somewhat surprised by the stark beauty of the area. During the years that he traveled for IBM, he had been privileged to go to such places as Paris, Rome, and London. This "business trip" of mine was quite different. A male nurse with whom I worked took him to Quinhagak to go fishing. He flew down in a plane with a "bush pilot" and learned first hand that when the wind changes off the Kuskokwim Bay, his jeans and jacket were not enough to keep him warm. He also learned that the wind also affects the swarms of large mosquitoes that gathered around his face looking for a tasty morsel. He did not catch many fish, but I think he enjoyed the experience.

I took a few days off, and we flew into Anchorage and visited the Indian Hospital where our patients were admitted when necessary. There, on a clear day, one can see the top of Mount McKinley, which is sometimes called Denali, meaning the "high one." This magnificent mountain rises more three miles above sea level, compared to Mount Everest which rises only 11,000 feet above the Tibetan Plateau.

I visited a patient I had evaluated for stomach cancer shortly after I arrived in Bethel and managed to have her admitted for treatment. She was surprised to see me, and I sensed her apprehension over her diagnosis and prognosis. She did not speak English to me, yet I know she understood more than she would admit. I saw her again when she returned to the hospital in Bethel in late June and was with her family when she died.

Carl and I rented a car to vacation on the Kenai Peninsula. Here we saw more of the beauty we had anticipated in Alaska. We visited glaciers, Cook Inlet, Homer, and the town of Seward. We stayed at a bed and breakfast in Homer and watched a mother moose and two of her young wander into a freshly plowed garden, obviously planning to return when the crops were in. While in Homer, we saw flocks of eagles! It was amazing to see so many of the birds that, not so long ago, were almost "extinct"! We went deep-sea fishing for halibut. I was unhappy when I had to throw back a thirty-pound halibut because it was "too small to keep"! It was all I could do to reel it in.

When I stepped out onto a glacier, I thought of one male nurse who told me with great excitement, that he had taken a holiday and "made love on a glacier"! Somehow, I had a little trouble with that image.

With this little vacation, one would think that the Bethel experience would fade in comparison with the areas of Alaska that tourists love so well. My quest was to deliver health care and study the people, their culture, their humor, and their coping skills. So I am glad that my first assignment was in Bethel, a more primitive and simple site that still speaks of the lives of the Native Alaskan people who have been there for so many centuries.

Reflections on
My First Assignment

As I complete this essay on my first assignment, there is much that I would like to share with you.

When I first arrived in Alaska, I did not see the beauty that is advertised in the travel brochures. There were no colorful totem poles, no exotic animals, no trees, and the population was sparse. The land appeared to be flat, and I might well have wondered whether I had arrived at the beginning of the earth's formation or at the end of the world. It was dusk, and there was no lovely display of colorful northern lights dancing across the sky, since it was not the right time of year. In fact, it was not a good time of the year. The drama of cold winter was about to end with the thawing of the mighty Kuskokwim River. With the thaw, the town and tundra revealed trash from last summer before the first snow.

The long days of the short growing season of summer were not yet upon us. It is said that on the Delta, one is always getting ready—getting ready for the next season, the thaw, the fishing, the short time for growing flowers and vegetables, and then getting ready for the winter, which is long and dark, but offers winter games, snowmobile events and other races, including the Iditerod, the most famous of Alaska's annual dogsled races. In 1994 the "mushers"—who train their dogs to pull their sleds across Alaska

from Metlakatla to Barrow, from Nunivak Island to Northway—
were in the race, which that year was billed as a "Race for
Sobriety." The racecourse stretched from Anchorage to Nome. The
Alaska Federation of Natives and others had organized the competition. Mike Williams, one of the participants, and others had collected signatures and pledges from well over ten thousand people
to raise money "to educate the young people and present them with
opportunities that become available when you're sober."

The tundra is full of drama, danger, and devastation. The earth
moves under your feet, and you feel unsure and remember reading
about giant animals that have frozen to death because they could
not pull themselves out of the muck. The tundra is rich when the
days are long; wild flowers and cultivated gardens produce color
and lush plants. The wild celery is as toxic as poison ivy is in the
South. Tomatoes and cabbages grow large rapidly.

In Bethel there are few mammals—an occasional fox, a wild
dog—but there are many birds that are a source of food for the
Native Alaskans. Salmon, herring, and whitefish give them both a
paycheck and subsistence.

This is a place where one can truly become a bird watcher and
a fisherman. The natives still eat the heart of the first fish they catch
or of any game that is the first kill of the season. And I do not mean
that they take it home and eat it. They immediately cut out the heart
and eat it raw. This is an act of thanksgiving and a request to the
gods for more of the same.

The beauty becomes apparent in the sky, the cloud formations,
the birds on the wing, and in the faces of the people. I was thrilled
by watching the ice break on the river, the logs come rushing down
from further north while men, women, and children rush to gather
the wood that is so rare in this part of the Delta. I was caught up in
sharing some of the excitement of the coming of spring.

I loved the work. I loved the people, the natives and my co-
workers. Despite the Yupik's quiet demeanor, their suspicions about
those of us who come for only a short while, and their reluctance to

Native children looking at pictures of my grandchildren, Bethel, Alaska (1994).

listen to our advice about their health and well-being, the kindness that I received was priceless.

On this journey, I started to study the humor of different cultures. You must watch their eyes. If they do not believe what you say or are displeased with your advice or action, they will not look at you at all. Once you have established a rapport, there are little smiles at the corners of their mouths, or more wrinkles around the eyes of the young and the old. As I mentioned before, they call those of us from the lower forty-eight "children of thunder" because we laugh and talk so loudly and are so excitable. There is a richness in the personalities born of hardship, true dependence on the earth and sea and whatever it may yield.

We in North Carolina and the rest of the lower forty-eight are spoiled by excess. We have so much to see, so much to do, so many opportunities to explore and experience. We are not aware of the simple beauties and blessings of life itself because our lives are so cluttered with television, movies, fast food, and noise. I left Alaska truly blessed by the simplicity of the land and the people.

Indiana

After my adventure in Bethel, imagine my response when I was asked to go to Columbus, Indiana, for a couple of months in August and September 1994. You can't. Was this a Native American reservation or a remote area? Were the patients needy?

None of the above was true. In Columbus, Indiana, there is a large company called Cummins Diesel. Yes, they make diesel engines. Cummins and another company in the area established a health clinic to provide physical examinations and other health resources to the employees. I had helped establish a healthcare center for a software corporation where I had worked for ten years before I retired. I was interested to see how this program provided similar services to its employees. I was only mildly interested in the assignment itself, performing physical examinations all day.

I had never been to Indiana, however, and took this opportunity to see this area of the state, with its beautiful cornfields surrounding Columbus. This city is often called "America's architectural showplace" because more than fifty public and private buildings, designed by some of the world's top architects, dot the city skyline. These world-class structures were designed by such notables as I.M. Pei, the Saarinens, Richard Meier, Skidmore-Owings and Merril, Harry Weese, and Robert A.M. Stern. The city has much civic pride and hosts a variety of cultural events supported by citizens who are determined to make their community the best.

Columbus had about thirty-two thousand residents in 1994. Cummins Engine Company was founded in 1919 in the city, which remains the site of its corporate headquarter and its largest engine manufacturing facility. In 1993, Cummins reported net sales of $4.2 billion and employed 23,600 people worldwide.

I was hired to do physical examinations on eight employees a day, all of whom were forty or more years old. Most of my patients were men. Most had never had a woman examine them. Therefore, my biggest challenge in this job was to make the men feel comfortable and to teach them how to improve or sustain their health. At times like this, professionalism is of utmost importance and to keep my humor appropriate and respect the patients was the rule of each day.

As in most healthcare institutions around the country in 1994, men were generally uninformed about the need to have an annual exam, to know about prostate health, and heaven forbid, to ask anyone about their sex life. This began to change after Robert Dole, Republican candidate for the United States presidency, was defeated by Bill Clinton. Dole began to make television commercials for Viagara, the wonder drug for "erectile dysfunction." Soon public discussion of a man's sex life, including that of President Clinton, began to be more acceptable.

Let me interrupt myself to tell you a little story. My friend, Joyce Neff, who is also a nurse practitioner, works in Louisburg, North Carolina. She records her medical notes into a voice-activated dictation system on the office computer. She had dictated that one of her patients had been diagnosed with erectile dysfunction. The system, however, understood her to say that the patient had "reptile dysfunction"!

Besides discussing all the physical maladies and preventive health measures that need to be addressed, I usually ask my patients about their work, what they do, how they enjoy it, etc. I do this because I like my work so well that I hardly think of patient care as work. I know that people who enjoy what they do are generally healthier, both physically and mentally. I must admit that, going in, I knew absolutely nothing about manufacturing engines and engine-related components, including turbochargers, filters, electronic control systems, heat-transfer equipment, electrical generators, and gasoline engines.

I remember one gentleman, obviously bored with his job, responding to my question with "I throw a rod all day!" Now this meant absolutely nothing to me, but I had a mental image of someone throwing a javelin, which obviously this is not how one "throws a rod." I asked him to consider that he was helping to build a great diesel engine. He looked at me and said, "Lady, I have never even seen a diesel engine."

When I inquired about their work, I had in mind the story about three men who were working on a building in Italy. Each man was asked what he was doing. The first man replied, "I am placing these stones beside one another." The second man replied, "I am building a wall." The third man replied, "I am building a great cathedral!" With the luxury of having a full hour with each patient, I wanted to consider all aspects of the patient's health. Needless to say, the man who had never seen a diesel engine and many of his co-workers were counting the days until their retirements.

I then began to ask what they did on their days off that made their lives enjoyable. Their answers ranged from fishing to farming or gardening to the strenuous activities of those who were more involved in physical fitness. I realized that, even in lovely towns with good health care and good health insurance, there are voids in our delivery of health care. Each time we see a patient, we must remind ourselves to look at the total person, the environment, the pitfalls, and the possibilities. We may be able to convey that good health is achieved, in part, by simply enjoying life—if not at work, then at play.

Some of the men were quite nervous about the rectal examination. One wife called, however, to thank me for helping her husband to address personal health problems in a positive way. I do a lot of teaching about prostate health before I do the examination. Then I perform that part of the exam so quickly that they are surprised how simple it was after all that dread. There were, of course, one or two who declined to have the exam, and I honored their preferences. I still did my teaching, and each went away with at least a little more understanding about his sexual health.

Land of Tall Corn and Sweet Watermelon

When I was a child, I saw the movie, *Oklahoma*. In it is a song with the lyric, "the corn is as high as an elephant's eye, and it looks like it's climbing clear up to the sky!" Now I have seen the beautiful tall corn with tassels blowing in the wind like spun gold. The cornfields of Indiana were that impressive.

On weekends, I traveled around the state to see some of the other places I had read about. I went to a watermelon festival in a small town, and the fruit was the sweetest that I have ever eaten. Of course, the festival was held around the town square, and the people were friendly. I realized that places, towns, villages, and even cities have personalities.

In Bethel, Alaska, there was a great deal of socializing in the waiting room of the outpatient department. When the patients came in, they often brought their baskets, soapstone pottery and traditional masks. Being ill provided them with an opportunity to show and sell their creative wares. If you go to a shop in Anchorage, the prices are greatly inflated, and there is no telling how much the artist actually receives from the shop sales. I decided then that any art objects I acquired would be purchased directly from the artist.

The watermelon festival reminded me of that decision. Most of the art consisted of crafts; clever storage bags in which you could save plastic grocery bags, wooden blocks for children, lampshades, etc. After all these years, I had no need or desire for these items. However, I enjoyed speaking to the artists and the vendors. It occurred to me that this is the sort of thing that people attend when they are not working and that there is much pleasure to be experienced in neighborhood events. We have the same sort of fairs and festivals all over the country.

In Cary, North Carolina, one of our big events is the "Lazy Days Festival," held in August. It has become so large that the artists are juried before they can participate. Fees must be paid, and the crowds are enormous. All through the day there are musical programs and so many food vendors. In the past, there were always corn dogs and soda pop. Now there are health foods, fruit cups, and vegetable pitas. The people, however, are the same.

Another place that I enjoyed was Madison, Indiana, a beautiful town on the Ohio River. I attended a junior college football game. The game was well played, and the crowds were respectful, sober, and having a great time. The land on the banks of the Ohio River is beautiful. Nestled in the picturesque Ohio River Valley, Madison, Indiana, was founded in the early nineteenth century as the major river port, railway center, and supply town outfitting pioneers moving into the Old Northwest Territory. Now its scenic waterfront, inviting shops, and rich architectural heritage offer visitors hours of pleasure, and the gardens are simply beautiful. I went with a new friend to Brownsville, Indiana, where there were many artisans, and we attended a play in the local barter theater. The play was *Once Upon a Mattress*, and it was funny and fun.

Why would I mention such things in a book about healthcare? Getting a look at the community in which I am working always helps me to know more about the people who live and work there. I have been asked why would I even bother to ask patients about their personal lives and the level of happiness that they may or may not have. And it is a valid question, when a health maintenance

organization has guidelines that allow you only ten to fifteen minutes per visit, to ask, "How can a provider possibly include such
information while they take a medical history?" After twenty-four
years as a nurse practitioner, I have found that such personal information can be a tremendous asset in discovering the strengths and
perhaps the voids in a patient's well being.

What more can I tell you about Indiana? The work was routine
and reasonably easy. The clinic did not treat any health problems.
When a problem was discovered, the patient was referred to an
appropriate physician. It seemed to me that it would be cost-effective and prudent to treat common colds, simple backaches, and perhaps a urinary-tract infection immediately and refer only if there
were no resolution.

Although there was little on-the-job excitement in this assignment, it was a time for me to observe the nature of a community of
people. It is true that if one has a repetitious job, like factory work
or data entry, there is not much excitement except when it is time
to go to lunch, go home at the end of the shift, or retire. That makes
it more important to find fulfillment and the joy of life after the
days' work.

Boston, Massachusetts

My original intent when I decided to travel was to work with Native American populations to study their cultures, including their humor. But I found myself associated with an agency that places nurse practitioners in many different settings across the country. In November 1994, such a call came. There was a need for a nurse practitioner to work at the Dana Farber Cancer Institute in Boston. DFCI, as it is called, is one of the leading cancer treatment and research centers in the United States. I had no oncology experience, but they wanted to interview me. Rarely does a hiring agency spend extra money for someone to be interviewed. But I got on a plane to Boston and met with some very exciting people who were involved in cancer research and treatment.

Despite my lack of experience with cancer patients, I have a world of experience doing physical exams. The folks in the breast-cancer center seemed to think that my skills were adequate, and they asked me to come to Boston. The two nurse practitioners in the breast-cancer clinic managed about fifty breast-cancer patients. One was going to take a maternity leave in a month or so, and they wanted someone to cover for her for four months. As intense as it seemed, I was excited to think of living in this vital city for the winter and early spring. And again, I wanted to learn how these patients and their families incorporated humor (or the lack of it) in dealing with this dreaded disease.

I reported to work on December 1 and was promptly sent to Sloan Kettering Hospital in New York City to learn about the latest cancer drugs. I took the train, an experience I had not had since I was a child in Tennessee when I would visit my grandmother. I thoroughly enjoyed the chance to travel this way again. People watching and seeing the northeastern coast of the United States was a real treat.

Sloan Kettering is located in a lovely section of the city. I took the bus to and from Grand Central Station, which was bustling with people going hither and yon. There were musicians and jugglers and someone who was preaching, prophesying that the end of the world was imminent, a message I have heard for at least fifty years. I have very little fear in strange places and a great deal of curiosity. The bus trip from the hotel—with old ladies sporting blue hair, sturdy shoes, and make-up that sometimes missed its mark—was fascinating. There was a beggar who was talking incoherently. I was told by one of the well-coifed blue-haired ladies that he was harmless. Every one of the passengers seemed to know each other. The driver made sure that I did not miss my stop. I saw young people walking as many as seven or eight dogs on leashes. I just could not imagine people having dogs in apartments or paying someone to walk the dog(s) with a herd of other neighborhood dogs. In the city, I really felt like a country bumpkin. New York caused me to gawk at the tall buildings. The class at Sloan Kettering was difficult, but the instructors were the type that wanted you to learn. They were not hard on us if we asked questions and revealed that we were ignorant about a certain drug or if we showed a lack of understanding of the curriculum.

Although Boston is a big city, I found it easy to get around. Of course, I turned in my rental car right away after I attempted to drive and then learned how simple it was to take a bus or subway. It was exciting to live in Boston. I lived in a sparsely furnished two-bedroom apartment. It was on the seventeenth floor, and I seemed to be the only person who took the stairs when there was a fire alarm, of which there were many, but thank God, no real fires. I walked to work every day, and in spite of the bitter cold, there was little snow in the winter of '94–'95. It was a short walk, and I found the people bundled up and hustling along to be fascinating. A verbally abrupt traffic cop with an Irish accent saw to it that I crossed the main street each day without getting run over by car or train.

Social life in Boston—what can I say? It is a wonderful city— one in which the history of our nation speaks to its visitors on the waterfront where the Boston Tea Party took place; at Faneuil Hall, a common meeting place with an adjacent Market, called the "Cradle of American Liberty" since many of the citizens and patriots met there after the Revolutionary war; the Old North Church, remembered for its connection with Paul Revere's ride; and many other historic sites. There are magnificent libraries, art museums, wonderful shops, and some of the finest restaurants in the world. I believe the best bread I have ever eaten was baked in Boston. It was easy to catch a subway and go over to Cambridge to visit the campus of Harvard University, browse the bookstores in Harvard Square, and watch the hungry sparrows come to your outdoor picnic on a park bench. Boston is a city full of young people, and no one seems to notice the cold. They just dress warmly, walk briskly through the streets, and go about their business without any sign of discomfort. One Sunday, I attended a Catholic church near my apartment where only Spanish was spoken. The hymns were lively and the old stone building was warmed by the enthusiasm of the congregation.

Carl came to visit me in Boston. Amy Frith, a delightful young woman who is the daughter of Carl's cousin, Charlie, took us out for a great seafood dinner. It was so good to get to know her better. She has lived in Boston for a long time and knows her way around. My daughters, Cindy and Becky, came up one weekend. We went to a bar and restaurant made famous in the TV sit-com, *Cheers*, and to Durgin Park, an old restaurant known for its Boston baked beans and the rudeness of its wait-staff. I once ordered a vegetable plate, and the waitress said to me, "What, you be grazing?" We took a weekend drive to Concord and Lexington to the see where the "shot heard round the world" was fired, signaling the start of the Revolutionary War. We also drove over to Pittsfield in the western part of the state to see where we lived when David, our son, was born. David visited at another time. When we lived in Pittsfield, Carl was working with General Electric. There were only a few places to rent in town. We took the small "shotgun" house (one room wide and three rooms long) because the other had two flights of stairs, and I was pregnant. At that time, it was badly in need of paint, but we were young and made it for almost a year, shoveled lots of snow, and moved back to the South before another full winter came along. The kids were somewhat shocked to see what a humble abode we lived in. To tell the story of our family moves and experiences would require another book.

My assignment was to work in DFCI's breast-cancer clinic. The nurse practitioners saw patients just like the physicians. When patients arrived for their appointments, they had laboratory work done, CAT scans, magnetic-resonance images (MRIs), or whatever was required for that visit. The most prevalent reason for the visit was to receive the prescribed chemotherapy or radiation treatment or to review the progress or diminishment of the cancer. There were protocols or standards of care determined by the patient's physician or group of physicians. These were determined by the type of cancer that the patient had—estrogen receptor, progesterone receptor, or metastatic (spread to bone, brain, lung, or other part of the body).

At each visit, the patient had a complete physical. The interview or history-taking told us how they were responding to therapy, what side effects they were experiencing, good or bad, and how they were managing emotionally. Many were able to continue working if they had chemotherapy on Friday with the weekend to recuperate. Many were out for a week or more every three to six weeks depending on their chemotherapy schedules. The patients went for the diagnostic testing, blood work, X-rays, etc. prior to our visit with them. The orders had been written at the previous visit. Sometimes orders were added as the result of phone consults or consultations with home-care nurses or hospice workers.

This was my first experience in using a computer to find lab results, history and physical notes, and doctor's orders or plans prior to seeing the patient. I also dictated my findings to be recorded on the computer. I am sure that by now providers are using voice-activated dictation. The responsibility that proved to be the most overwhelming for me was to determine if all of the criteria had been met for a chemotherapy treatment. I never wrote an order for chemotherapy without a consultation with the oncologist. There were some orders that I wrote in regard to nausea and pain medicine. Even those were written according to protocol.

Despite the fact that the nurse practitioners were extremely bright and caring, it seemed to me that providing this level of care—not to mention admitting patients into the hospital when needed—was equal to that of an attending physician or a fellow. Imagine how I felt when both nurse practitioners left their jobs by the end of December. I called the agency to say that I could not possibly do this job. The absence of the nurse practitioners left me with responsibilities beyond my scope of practice. The director of the breast-cancer clinic was also quite distraught about the situation. After much thought, I went to tell him what I did feel comfortable doing. I would not take call, admit patients, or write orders for hospitalized patients or for protocols without physician review. I was still expected to evaluate lab results, CAT scans, and MRIs, and we came to an agreement that my duties would remain within the limits of my comfort zone.

It was my good fortune that a bright young nurse, Kerri Scholl, was reassigned to work with me. She is an excellent oncology nurse. She had never worked in the breast-cancer clinic before, but had worked in the oncology unit in the hospital, where many breast-cancer patients were treated. She also new the ins and outs of the hospital, the people who worked in the various departments, and how to access many services.

It was such a treat for me to work with her and to get to know her. She is energetic, smart, and somewhat fearless. In fact, her bold questions to the physicians caused me to ask her one day, "Have you ever been written up for being sassy?" She thought this was hysterical. Once again, I realized how much things have changed since I was a young nurse. After all, we were taught to take orders, to stand up when a physician appeared, and not to ask too many questions.

Kerri was, and I am sure still is, quite beautiful. She had long, black, curly hair that was somewhat untamed. I dubbed her "Medusa" after the mythical goddess who had snakes for hair. She was amused by that nickname. We had a great working relationship as well as a rich friendship for the rest of my assignment.

Despite my responsibility for all of these duties, I was also able to learn how humor aided in the patients' lives.

Humor and Cancer

How can there be any humor when one is facing such a devastating and frightening disease as cancer? Many factors can make a difference in the attitude that a patient has when a crisis occurs. Through the years when I think of my own experiences with cancer or those of many of my patients, there are traits or attitudes that contribute to the course of the disease from diagnosis to treatment and, perhaps, even to outcome. For example, what is the patient's personality? Is the patient negative or positive about life in general? Is the patient well educated and more knowledgeable about the disease than the average person? In the Information Age, can most folks just look things up on the Internet and draw their own conclusions? It used to be that we, as providers, were challenged by patients who had read articles in *Ladies Home Companion* or similar magazines. Now they bring us pages of information that seem to make sense, yet do not always contain accurate information. Of course, there are those who have had the experience of having friends and family who have had positive outcomes and/or devastating losses with the big "C"!

It is difficult to explain this phenomenon without sharing my own personal experience with cancer. In 1975, a nodule was discovered on my thyroid. I had had a benign cyst removed in 1958, so I was not concerned. However, after surgery to remove the nodule on my thyroid in 1975, my doctor was surprised to find that the nodule was a thyroid cancer. Fortunately, he had removed it all, leaving me with one half of the gland in place. He assured me that, with proper medication, the possibility of a recurrence would be remote. Despite the good news, I heard the word *"cancer"* loud and clear. I was to turn forty years old in a few months, and I began to think that I should live my life as if each day were a gift. I had been encouraged to go to University of North Carolina's School of Nursing to become a family nurse practitioner. I loved hospital nursing and was a little leery of returning to an academic program at the age of forty. My oldest child was going to be a senior in high school. My two other children were in seventh and tenth grades and participated in many extracurricular activities. The government, however, would pay my tuition if I had a job waiting for me at the end of the year. What does having cancer have to do with this? For me, it was a kick in the pants, telling me to go for it, not to pass up this opportunity. That decision has been one of the best of my life.

The cancer did not return until 1988, which necessitated a total thyroidectomy. We now know that the radiation treatments I received in my teen years for eczema on my face probably contributed to the cancer. But that was an accepted practice in the fifties, so I saw no need to pursue any legal action seeking restitution for my thyroid cancer. Over the years, as we study the etiology (or causes) of cancer, medical researchers have discovered that environmental agents often play a large part in its occurrence. But the complete picture is much more complex than that. The patient who gets cancer also has certain genetic and other traits that can make one person more vulnerable than others. We know that smoking, obesity, and a high level of alcohol consumption can make one more vulnerable. That does not explain why, when people who take excellent care of themselves, have no genetic history of cancer, no risk factors, and positive personalities also get this disease.

Over the years, I have practiced "the art of nursing" enough to know that there is no value added in discussing just how one gets cancer or in placing blame. It just seems to make matters worse for both the patients and their families. I know it is tempting to say, "See, I told you so. You should never have smoked those nasty cigarettes." That lesson needs to be taught to our children before they ever take that first dare or that first drag. Once the disease is there, the patient has already figured out what may have made them a "victim" of cancer. If they have not done anything that seemed to contribute to their cancer, many will decide that it is just bad luck; others will ask the unanswerable question, "Why me?"; and still others will conclude that it is God's will. We know a great deal about the etiology of disease, but we may never have all of the answers.

At DFCI, I managed fifty breast-cancer patients for the next three months. Some of my more memorable patients were:

- The young mother who gave birth to both of her children after she had been diagnosed and treated. She died when the youngest was fifteen months old. Her devoted husband expected her to die, but it did not assuage his devastation. He did have the little girls that they had wanted so much. It cannot be easy for him. The mother's humor and happy times centered on her children and the wide array of hats she had collected during the six years she had breast cancer.

- There was the mother of five who had lived for ten years with a variety of treatment protocols until she decided that enough was enough. Her fear was that her decision to stop chemotherapy would, as she said, "disappoint my doctor," the physician whose care had brought her this far. Personally, I do believe that a patient has the right to decide when enough is enough. But we talked about the quality of her life during the past ten years, the laughter of her children, and the support of her husband and family, and we cried over her acceptance that this would be her last Christmas with them. She wanted to be free of nausea, to go Christmas shopping, to enjoy what little hair had grown back, and to eat lots of turkey and coconut pie.

- Another was the sixty-seven-year-old woman who cried when her doctors told her that there was no new protocol, no new medicine that could change this final course of her cancer. She and her daughters—so faithful over the twelve years of her illness—counted their blessings and faced the final outcome with courage and support for their mom.

- I also met a thirty-nine-year old woman who was between chemotherapy treatments and wanted so much to have a fulfilling and satisfactory lovemaking weekend with her husband. The medicine had caused profound vaginal dryness, and she was anorgasmic. I encouraged her to buy some Astroglide (a water-based lubricant that was invented for the space program and subsequently found suitable for intravaginal use) and then take her husband to a romantic bed-and-breakfast for the weekend. She returned the next week, having had a wonderful time, but she had developed what we call "honeymoon cystitis." That was okay. We could treat that very common problem with a little antibiotic prescription.

- There was a forty-five-year-old Portuguese woman who told fortunes. She loved to tell my fortune and give me "lucky numbers" for the lottery. I wondered why she never was lucky with numbers herself, so I never bought a lottery ticket. Her cancer had grown outside of her chest, and it was devastating for her to look at herself and see the growing mass that was her enemy. It was like watching a horror movie. But she still found laughter and gave much love to those of us who were caring for her. One of her treatments involved freezing the tumor over many hours to treat it with drugs that would slow its growth.

- Another woman, fifty-five years old, was Hispanic. She owned a beauty shop just outside of Boston, wore beautiful wigs, and had a beautiful spirit. Her cancer had spread to her abdominal cavity, filling it with fluid that needed to be drained periodically. She was thin and lovely, but with all that fluid inside, she looked eight months pregnant. Her oncologist would bring her in to tap the belly and draw off the fluid. As with most of these patients, she loved her doctor, brought gifts to him and teased him. They were as much friends as they were doctor and patient. She was laughing with him one day when he was going to draw the fluid off. First, he had to perform an ultrasound to be sure where he could place the large needle, or cannula, and not hit a vital organ. As he was washing his hands, he realized that he was not using the soap from the dispenser: he was attempting to wash his hands with ultrasound jelly. Ordinarily, he was a pretty serious fellow, but the patient and I had a great laugh over this, and he knew that, with me there, this story would eventually find its way into print.

There are many untold stories. Patients need pain medicine, especially toward the end, and we made it available to them. Pain medicine makes one very constipated. You can imagine the glee patients experience when we provide a laxative that gives them relief from yet another discomfort. They made many jokes about using lactulose, a very effective laxative, when they described their relief upon expelling the "mother lode."

The patients and nurses shared many stories during chemotherapy treatments—stories of families, feelings, and frustration. All of them appreciated the nurses who administered their medications, who were and are skilled and compassionate while caring for patients who suffer so much that the time any provider would spend with them in the supportive atmosphere of DFCI seemed like a profound relief. These nurses are truly Health Heroes.

But no matter how "good" an institution is, sometimes tragedy strikes.

Tragedy Strikes

For years, I have presented humor programs to patients, nurses, doctors, and anyone who wants rejuvenation. I felt that I had something to offer at DFCI in that regard. I had planned to present such a program at Grand Rounds, but someone said, "It is not a good time for that."

I learned why the next day. All of the doctors, fellows, and nurse practitioners were called into a meeting. A woman in her forties had died from an overdose of adriamycin, one of the chemotherapy agents that was being administered prior to a bone-marrow transplant. She happened to work for the *Boston Globe*, writing a regular column on health issues. Her husband worked at DFCI. A bone-marrow transplant is often the last available treatment to rid the body of breast cancer. As the director told us the story, you could hear a pin drop in that room full of over one hundred people. The orders had been written stating the amount of adriamycin to be administered over the course of four treatments; the orders had been misinterpreted, and as a result, the patient had been given four times too much in a single dose. Because this drug has a profound effect on the heart as well as the tissue in one's intestines and other internal organs, the patient had died. How could this have happened?

There were investigations into the protocol, the pharmacy, the doctor, the nurses who administered the drug, and the system itself.

There were resignations and some dismissals. DFCI lost its accreditation for a while. The patients, however, were supportive and loyal to the hospital and their respective caregivers. As for the silence in the meeting, each of us was thinking, "It could have been me who made this fatal mistake."

Patients who are diagnosed with cancer want the best: the best doctors, the best nurses, the best support system and accuracy, as well as caring people. Most of the time, this is what they get. And then there is a mistake. It could happen to any of us. That is why it is so important to me to have a consulting colleague and physician who works with me and corrects me when I could be taking the wrong path to healing for the patient.

As nurse practitioners, we all seek autonomy at times. That is good when we feel competent as well as caring. For me, the team approach to care in cancer therapy, family practice, and emergency situations is ideal. In this tragic Boston case, the fatal error was discovered by a clerk who examines the records to insure that treatment protocols are being followed. A protocol is written as a plan for treatment that is decided upon by research physicians who are starting treatment plans, ordering all of the appropriate diagnostics tests, and writing the orders for the pharmacy to fulfill their prescriptions with the correct drug and dosage, which then goes to the chemotherapy nurses who administer them. At each step of the way, nurses, pharmacists, nurse practitioners, and physicians must be aware of the protocol guidelines. Any member of the team could make a mistake.

On my next assignment, I found myself to be the lone healthcare provider on the island of Ocracoke on North Carolina's Outer Banks. Teamwork in this setting was also quite challenging.

Ocracoke, North Carolina

Spring was approaching. It was time for me to leave Dana Farber Cancer Institute and Boston. I received a call from the North Carolina Department of Health, asking me to work in Ocracoke for a couple of months. After the cold winter and short days in Boston, I was excited to go south and work on an island. Ocracoke is the southernmost island of North Carolina's Outer Banks. It is one of the few islands that has retained its '40s and '50s charm.

My reflections of May 27, 1995, recall fond memories. I wrote:

> The oleander is blooming all over the island and in the front yard of the Parker cottage, where I am staying. When I carried my parcels in, the wooden screen door slammed behind me. The cottage is modest, the furnishings reminiscent of those cast aside by family members as they remodeled their homes in permanent abodes in other, more modern cities and towns.

> The cottage has its own distinct character and personality. I seem to feel the presence of former inhabitants, and if their ghosts are here, they are kind and hospitable spirits. I understand that the owners purchased the house on this remote island in the 1950s. There is a faded photograph on the living room wall that includes a car and a pickup truck of that era. There are no trees in the photo, but there is an old picket fence. The cottage has a fine porch swing, a barn with

a washer and dryer, and a clothesline. I am very nostalgic about clotheslines. When I hang the linens out to dry my memory is flooded by the sweet smell of fresh air and of cloth diapers that I have hung outside throughout the years.

The longer I stay, the more I learn about the history (truth or fable) of the cottage. I was told it was first used as a fishing-and-hunting club and that only male members of the families who owned the property visited here. I also heard that the man who owned the cottage built fine hunting rifles. I discovered a 1908 Sears Roebuck catalog to browse through. There is another house on the island that was built from a kit ordered from this catalog. [Ed.—My mom grew up in a house that her father built from a Sears Roebuck kit; everything, from floor joists to shingles, was delivered in four or five (horse-drawn) wagonloads.]

Now the yard is full of sweet clover, a few fig trees, a maple tree, and the gnarled evergreen trees bent by the ever-present wind and the storms of years gone by. There are neat flowerbeds bordered by seashells. The beds are filled with blooming prickly pear cactus, impatiens, primrose, and hollyhock. There are old-fashioned tea roses that run along the board fence out near the road.

When I step out the back door onto the painted steps, I see the lighthouse only a few yards away above the trees and brush. It is only seventy-five feet tall and has a more squatty than stately appearance. It is still functional and from here, its light seems almost dim, and I wonder what the crewmen on the ferries and in their private boats see when they approach the island between dusk and dawn. The water tower on the north shore of the island is taller, and it is the first structure that one sees on the horizon across Pamlico Sound whether one arrives from Cedar Island south of Ocracoke or from Swan Quarter on the eastern edge of the mainland.

Now to describe this setting in more general terms: Most of the long-time inhabitants of Ocracoke Island are descendants of four families. They still speak the language of those "down-east" folks and sound like they just arrived from England. Ocracoke is a town of legends: Blackbeard and his ghost; the story that the fig trees only bear if someone is living in the house where the trees are planted; and stories of the many hurricanes and floods that have visited the island. While hurricanes and tourists may come and go, the permanent residents rarely leave. They rely on the tourist industry for their livelihoods, but they have resisted high-rise condos, miniature golf courses, and would like to do away with automobiles, since most prefer boats, bikes, and ferries as transportation. In fact, the only way to get a car onto the island is to take it there on a ferry. There is also a small airport where independent pilots are more than willing to transport the braver folks.

The Health Department Clinic is the only healthcare facility on the island. The physician's assistant (PA) had left two months before, and they needed someone to take-on the PA's workload until a full-time replacement could be hired. The nurse, secretary-receptionist, and I were the only employees. The nurse did the lab work, assisted me, and filled the prescriptions that I wrote or those written by other doctors that the residents needed refilled. They had a few over-the-counter drugs that folks could buy. One of these was a cough medicine that contains codeine. Fortunately, the nurse and receptionist knew the people who came in for cough medicine on a regular basis. The previous provider was a male PA. He was quite competent and had a good reputation. Yet, as soon as the word was out that a female nurse practitioner was working at the clinic for a while, dozens of women scheduled appointments for pap smears and gynecological exams. The older women in town had just put these exams off for the eight years that the PA had been there. This is not to say that everyone waited; most of those whom I saw were over fifty years old.

As for the humor in the practice:

- A delightful seventy-five-year-old lady came in for a physical and wanted a pap smear. The receptionist rolled her
  eyes when she made the appointment. The patient and I got
  along just dandy, and I asked her if she wanted to play a little joke on the receptionist. She agreed. When she was
  checking out with the receptionist, I asked her if she needed her prescription for birth-control pills refilled. The receptionist looked shocked, and then we had a good laugh.

Most of the visits were from tourists who had developed colds,
had small lacerations, bad sunburns, or rashes. Many residents and
tourists came in for evaluation of chronic diseases, such as diabetes
and high blood pressure. For patients who have a variety of
providers, it must be difficult for a new person to suggest a change
in the medication or treatment; that may be a new experience for
them. It's not that most of us do not practice according to accepted
standards of care; it is just that one provider may have had a good
experience with a drug that is new on the market or one that has
been around for a long time and is much less expensive.

At least four people with chest pain came to the clinic while I
was there. My consulting physician was in Cape Hatteras, and he
was always available by phone and helped me through diagnosis,
treatment, and referral. Just as in Alaska, sometimes a decision
needed to be made about how a patient should be transported to the
proper institution for special care: by helicopter, plane, boat, or
ferry. At that time, Ocracoke had only one ambulance and two or
three EMTs, but no paramedics or special equipment on the vehicle.

- One day, the emergency folks brought a woman was into
  the clinic from a ferry. Two nurses, who happened to be passengers on the ferry, noted that a man was concerned
  because he could not wake his wife in their car. They discovered that she had no pulse, and they began CPR. The

ferry crew called the Coast Guard, who transported an EMT to the ferry; the EMT continued resuscitation until the patient arrived at the clinic. There was no doubt that the woman had died. Her husband was with her, and the rest of the family had to be notified. The body was transported to the mainland and then to her home. How sad to lose a loved one while on vacation.

(In 2002, a new hospital was opened in Hatteras, which is on the island just north of Ocracoke. What a blessing!)

The hours at the clinic were a little unusual. We saw patients from 8:00 a.m. until 1:00 p.m. The clinic then closed until 3:00 p.m., when we opened again until 7:00 p.m. It was nice to have a break in the middle of the day on this lovely island. The experience of the clinic was that people did not come in during the early afternoon. After reopening at 3:00, we saw most of the trauma and acute-care patients.

- The worst trauma victim that I saw was a seventeen-year-old boy who had gone surfing in the early afternoon and hit a wave that caused him to almost swallow one end of his surfboard. He kept after me to just sew the roof of his mouth up so he could return to his job in a local restaurant. There was no way! I was sure that he had also fractured the roof of his mouth, and his jaw had a large laceration and many loose teeth. I was able to contact an oral surgeon and send him on his way. The next day, in Greenville, North Carolina, he had surgery, and his jaw was wired for several weeks. Needless to say, he did not make it back to his job or to surfing that summer.
- Another evening, the nurse said, "There is a man coming in with a lacerated scalp!" I was not too concerned. A lacerated scalp bleeds profusely but rarely needs stitches. Then I heard, "He is a surgeon from Raleigh!" and I began to get a

little nervous. The next voice I heard was that of a very respected and beloved surgeon whom I had known for several years. I told him, "Oh, my, I can't sew you up!" Dr. Yarborough kindly assured me that he was glad he knew me and that I would be the perfect one to sew up his wound. He was not so pleased that he needed a tetanus shot, but that was accomplished without too much argument. I reviewed the procedure with him, saying that I would numb the scalp very well and would take my time. He replied, "Jimmie, just take all the time you want." His next question was, "Jimmie, how much of this wound is in my hairline?" Reluctantly I replied, "Not enough!" You see, this young doctor was prematurely bald, with only a fringe of hair around the lower back of his head. He had slipped on some fish slime as he got out of his boat and hit his head right in the middle of his posterior scalp.

By the next time that I saw him, I had discovered my breast lump, and we were planning the biopsy. I asked him to let me see his head before we scheduled the surgery. Fortunately, he had great skin, and there was only a very fine scar.

Many boats came to Silver Lake, Ocracoke's harbor. The semi-circular harbor was home to many sailboats, fishing vessels, and the Coast Guard house. The lovely, scenic harbor has been the subject of many paintings over the years. My time on the island was a good time to sail, to go to the beach looking for treasures, like interesting pieces of driftwood, and to paint pictures of the lighthouse and the harbor.

I have described my 1994 experiences in Bethel, Alaska, and there are interesting similarities between these two places. Both are fishing villages, both are remote, and both are inhabited by people who are familiar and comfortable with their family histories. The experiences of both groups of people have been shaped by their environment and by their fierce independence. The cultures of both lifestyles speak to me of a survival that has been challenged by the weather and to some extent by what others of us may have viewed as poverty or, at best, limited resources.

Neither the Yupik nor the "Ocracokers," as they call themselves, seem to think of themselves as poor. As I provided service to them in the healthcare facilities, I sensed that they feel comfortable in these settings that recall their rich heritages. They respect their ancestors and appreciate the natural resources that the land, sea, and rivers provide.

In both settings, I was first received with skepticism and then with appreciation for whatever time I could devote. There are a variety of reasons why healthcare providers do not stay in these remote areas. It takes a special kind of person to live in a small village where everyone knows every move you make. There is no privacy, and the inhabitants feel free to call upon you at any time of the day or night, just as one's family might. "Burnout" is the term one hears over and over from those caregivers who have spent between two and ten years in such an environment. For some of us, "burnout" occurs in big cities, where salaries are much more generous, and the facilities are much more contemporary.

This "big-city" burnout is usually the result of long hours and stress.

In 1994 and 1995, I worked in the heartland of America, in a modern occupational-health facility teaching the folks in Columbus, Indiana, about their bodies and encouraging them to make healthy decisions. I had worked in Boston, a bustling city of medicine, caring for breast-cancer patients from all over the world. I met healthcare providers in every setting who professed that they suffered from "burnout." This prompted me to ask then, and I still ask, *"Why?"* In my own experience, it seems that experiencing burnout has a lot to do with whether we are doing what we really do best. For me, that seems to be direct patient care—not management, not consulting, not even professional speaking. For me, the essence of any of the success that I may have experienced in all other endeavors depends wholly on the experience that I gain from my direct involvement with patients.

A common theme prevails in this variety of setting. I have cared for uneducated and poor patients; I have cared for well-educated and well-to-do patients. I have experienced both the worst and the best healthcare facilities. The common theme of which I speak is the sincere and respectful attitude we communicate to our patients.

To be successful, happy, and to avoid burnout, we must seek to find the right fit professionally, to be astute technically, and through our performance, to convey to our patients that we truly care for them. We must treat them as individuals who not only deserve to be well cared for, but who also deserve the opportunity to become an active participant in their health care.

There are two phrases that I can relate to in my career. Oliver Wendell Holmes said that life is a romance and that it up to us to make the romance by having the passion for life, which he described as "having fire in your belly!"

The second phrase has to do with being "easy in your harness." That is, all of us must be comfortable operating or performing within certain guidelines.

Therefore, besides having a passion for what we do, we may avoid burnout by anticipating the enormity of the tasks that we must perform and somehow getting prepared for the inevitable when we are overwhelmed. This is all easier said than done. I am grateful that my experience in this career has been that I have found both the passion for life and the assurance of being easy in my harness.

Sand Point in the
Aleutian Islands, Alaska

In August 1995, I was asked to work for a month in the Aleutian Islands. There is an Indian Health Clinic there, and at that time, the clinic was staffed by two community health aides (CHAs), a receptionist, and a social worker. They did a very good job of taking care of the inhabitants, mostly Aleuts, without a physician or nurse practitioner. During the fishing season, however, the population doubles, as folks from Japan, Hawaii, and the lower forty-eight come to work in the fishery for the season. The clinic could benefit by seeing these patients who had insurance other than the Indian Health Service payment. In order to charge these patients, it was required that a licensed provider see them.

Sand Point is on the Popoff Island and has nine hundred permanent residents. Eighty per cent of them work for the Peter Pan Seafood Processing Plant. In winter, they fish for crab, pollock, and cod. In the summer, they fish for salmon and halibut. There were huge lobster crates everywhere, but the lobsters had been fished out. The island has an active volcano and has suffered severe earthquakes in the past. One of the first things that I received instruction on was the emergency plan for a possible tsunami. My lessons included knowing the hazard zones and how to transfer the clinic to the school high on the mountaintop.

My consulting physician worked at the Indian hospital in Anchorage, 650 miles east of Sand Point. My assignment was to work in the clinic each day Monday through Friday and to be on-call twenty-four hours a day, seven days a week for this one month.

The work was both challenging and rewarding. During regular office hours, I saw fisherman who had come in from their work with sore backs, lacerations, and upset stomachs. I saw some of the natives who needed more evaluation than the CHAs were able to perform. But I think the CHAs just needed confirmation from me of what they had already figured out. We were also busy restocking supplies and doing housecleaning, as well as performing prenatal visits, well-child checks, and paperwork. All pregnant women from remote areas are sent to Anchorage for their ninth month of pregnancy and delivery. This practice has been found to decrease infant mortality.

On weekends, commercial fishing was restricted, and everybody was back in the village. Those who had waited until the weekend to take care of their medical needs came in with twisted ankles, sore muscles, prescriptions for chronic

The walk from my apartment to the clinic in Sand Point, Aleutian Islands, Alaska (1995).

medication that needed refilling, and the conditions that resulted from continuing episodes of alcohol-related incidents, which always seemed to occur in the middle of the night.

A few stories will demonstrate the challenge of being in a remote area with limited medical resources:

- The police brought me an eleven-year-old girl. She suffered from some degree of mental retardation due to a head injury she had sustained when she was younger. On this day, she was riding a boy's multi-speed bike, and in her attempt to stop it, she fell on the bar, injuring her perineum.

  Because the child had been approached two days before by a twelve-year-old male playmate asking to have sex, the mother called the police when she realized that her daughter was bleeding from her vagina and crying in pain. My first task was to make full assessment of her injuries. This was complicated because of the pain and swelling. She had had a number of hospitalizations in regard to the previous head injury. Ideally, she needed intravenous sedation in order for me to perform a complete examination. Neither the CHA nor I could start the IV. Her veins were poor, her mother was impatient, and the child was hysterical. We did administer sedation intramuscularly, which meant having to wait thirty minutes to complete the exam. I was quite busy and notified my consulting physician in Anchorage about the extent of her injuries, including the development of a large hematoma (the size of a small apple) on her vulva from the bleeding. I needed to question the mother in regard to the possibility of sexual assault, and if that was determined to be the cause of her injuries, I needed to notify protective services. And if sexual assault was a possibility, I needed to proceed with the proper steps to document the assault. The policeman who brought them in was waiting for me to decide. If sexual assault is determined, there are about sixteen steps that must be taken prior to and during the examination to confirm whether or not the victim has been truly assaulted.

Besides caring for her physical situation, we had to locate the sexual-assault kit, the Polaroid camera, and have certain papers signed. I learned that in the state of Alaska it is not a crime if an eleven- or twelve-year-old has intercourse. For it to be a crime, the male must be at least three years older than the female. (I did not learn if the reverse were true.) The girl denied that there had been intercourse; she was crying and saying that she knew that her mother was refusing to believe the real story. Ultimately, no one wanted to press charges, so there was no need to pursue the assault possibility.

Because of the extent of her injuries, I determined that the young girl needed to be under the care of a gynecologist in Anchorage. She needed to travel with a medical escort, and the CHA went with her at the expense of the Indian Health Service. Fortunately, the incident occurred at a time when she could fly commercially at a cost of $800, versus $10,000 for Medivac or $13,000 for a chartered flight. The weather cooperated, and we learned that a commercial plane was leaving within the hour. There was the additional $800 for the medical escort plus her food and lodging for two nights until a flight would be returning to the island on Monday, but the total was far less than the alternatives, and the CHA would only miss one day of work! It sounds rather mercenary of me to mention the financial aspect of this situation, but in today's environment of escalating healthcare costs, it needs to be said.

I want to comment on the helpfulness of everyone who was involved. I was a stranger in this land. The important players in this scenario are the local health practitioners and aides, the local police officers, the consulting physician (in Anchorage), and those who know the culture and mores of this community.

It is said that all's well that ends well. This young girl was delivered safely into the care of a kind woman gyne-cologist and anesthesiologist (the emergency room person-nel could not get an IV started either) and a proper exam and skilled treatment were performed. After twenty-four hours in the hospital, she was discharged and returned on the same flight as the CHA.

• Another story involves a sixteen-year-old girl who was walking on the handrail of a footbridge at one o'clock on a Sunday morning. She fell twenty feet onto rocks and mud. She was brought to me on a stryker stretcher with blood pouring from a scalp wound. The X-ray equipment in the clinic was limited and could not take cervical spine and back films. During my careful assessment to prevent further injury, the girl sat up on the stretcher when her inebriated father and his equally inebriated woman friend got into a verbal altercation. The girl sat up to "set them both straight." There was obviously no paralysis. She was even-tually discharged from the clinic to be seen in Anchorage at the Indian Hospital on Monday and since she had already planned a vacation trip to Anchorage, there was no trans-portation cost to Indian Health Service. The worst part of this encounter was the argument about where to go that Sunday morning. She was living on a boat with her father, but she opted to go home that night with his woman friend. With all of this confusion about who was the more reliable of the two, I was concerned that no one understood my instructions about the need to observe a patient closely, fol-lowing a head injury, to watch for signs of serious compli-cations, such as increased confusion, severe headache, inability to wake the patient, etc.!

When one is working on a small island, there are only so many miles that a person can travel. This next story did allow me a bit of humor, although the incident itself was not funny.

• There is a van that takes fishermen from the cannery ship (there is no permanent factory on shore) to the airport, which is about ten miles away. Two men had been fired from the cannery because they had been intoxicated on the job. The van driver, an energetic little fellow, was transporting them to the airport for their trip home. There was a young woman in the van, as well. The men began harassing the woman. To protect her, the driver stopped the van, warning the men that if they didn't behave, he would call the local police. One of the drunks then attacked the driver with a ballpoint pen, striking the driver in the neck. Then he threw everyone out of the van and drove away.

Meanwhile, in the clinic, we could hear every police call and every transmission on the island. We heard the van driver call the police to say that his van had been hijacked. The police picked up the driver and brought him to the clinic for medical attention. His injury was superficial. When it was all over, I was amused to think about a van being hijacked on this island, where there were only a few miles of road to travel! We all got a chuckle, thinking, "Where the heck did the perpetrator think he would go?" The hijacker managed to evade the police for about an hour before he crashed the van.

As I have said so many times, my nursing career has never been boring. My friends on the island made my assignment quite pleasant. I was invited to their homes for dinner. I took a class at the high school and learned to make dream catchers, a native work of art that is designed to hang over a child's bed to capture any bad dreams before they have a chance to enter the child, thereby assuring them a peaceful sleep. Marcy Landreth and Ingrid Carlson, my co-workers at the clinic, talked me into riding a four-wheel-drive all-terrain vehicle to the top of the island's mountain, where we saw an eagle's nest containing young eagles on a cliff just over the ocean. We could also see the area where some buffalo roam; yes, buffalo!! They were brought to the island many years ago from the mainland, and each year the island's inhabitants hold a buffalo hunt. I was told that a family of grizzly bears also lived on the island. I was not told how they got there! The ride up the mountain was exhilarating, to say the least. It was brisk and sunny, and the air was sweet and clean. I could hardly have imagined doing such a thing after I was sixty years old.

By the way, the aides also gave all of the local pets their immunizations, and if a sick animal had to be euthanized, they performed this task with love and support for owner(s) of the pet. The islanders love their dogs, and they love them to be big. When I asked if my Yorkie could have come with me, I was told that any animal that weighed less than fifty pounds just might be carried off by an eagle. The month passed quickly. I returned to Cary, North Carolina, and felt as if I had entered a steam bath when I stepped off the plane. Despite much work, there is more ahead. Read on!

Riding a four wheel ATV to see the eagle nest on Popoff Island
in the Aleutian Islands, Alaska (1994).

Back to Massachusetts

After returning to Cary, North Carolina, from the Aleutian Islands, I got a call requesting that I take an assignment at the University of Massachusetts at Amherst (UMA). They wanted someone to work as a family nurse practitioner or physician's assistant for the entire school year. Someone had applied for the position, but it would be a month before the "approval to practice" could be completed, and I was still approved to work in Massachusetts, making me a perfect candidate to fill in for a month or so.

Knowing that nearby Vermont and western Massachusetts would be flooded with brilliant fall colors in the Berkshire and Green Mountains (if only for a few days, since that area's brief summer is followed by three rapturous days of fall, and then comes winter!), I took the assignment.

I left on September 6 to stay until October 1. I worked in at the Student Health Center Urgent Health Care Clinic from 10:00 p.m. until 8:00 a.m., four nights a week. At that time, there were twenty-three thousand students enrolled at UMA. The Health Care Center also served the healthcare needs of three to four thousand students from nearby Hampshire College and Amherst College, as well as three thousand Kaiser Permanente Health Plan members, who were mostly faculty, staff, and their families.

I sutured more alcohol-related lacerations during "rush week" than I did during both assignments in Alaska. We may read a lot about alcohol-related illness and injuries in the Native Alaskan culture, but they certainly do not surpass what happens on the campuses of some of our colleges and universities.

I also prescribed more "morning-after" birth-control pills than I would have ever imagined. Many of the condoms sold in Massachusetts must be of extremely poor quality since so many of them "broke," and the women greatly feared pregnancy. Of course, I think that many of the condoms never got out of the participants' pockets or dresser drawers. I had just about decided that I certainly did not want any of my grandchildren to go to school in that setting. To be fair, however, I should attempt to be objective: I imagine that many of students whom I saw were not representative of the majority of people who attend these prestigious institutions.

My impression was that these eighteen-to-twenty-year-old "children" were off at a Halloween party, dressed in leather and tattooed, with all the fleshy parts of their bodies pierced in some way. I saw pierced ears, eyebrows, noses, lips, and navels—the worst was a huge spike through a young lady's tongue! As I write this, it is 2002, and I see the same things in Cary, North Carolina. I guess it just takes a while for some styles and fashions to spread into the South. Now many students here decorate themselves with collars and chains, "jewelry" originally intended for dogs.

I was to stay in the private home of a woman who worked in the university's administration. A graduate student, a gentleman about my age, was in one of the three small bedrooms. I was in another, and the owner had the master bedroom. We all shared one bath and had kitchen privileges. All of this was okay, yet at my age, I am more accustomed to privacy and a bit more space. When I arrived, no one was at home. The door was unlocked, and I went in to make sure that I was in the right place and to make myself at home. I read some of the material posted on the refrigerator door. There was a list of rules for "guests of this establishment." They included: "Do not leave the grounds beyond the fences. Do not take photos without written permission of the patrons. Always take a towel to sit on," etc., etc., etc. I finally figured out that the landlady was a nudist. When she drove in, I saw on her car a bumper sticker that read, "Happiness is no tan lines!" She was about my age and although attractive enough, no raving beauty. The "rules" I had read were not for this abode. They were for a nudist colony out on Cape Cod, which she visited on weekends. This was yet another new experience for me. I moved in on Sunday and out on Wednesday!

I found a motel room with a small kitchen in Northampton, which is a very interesting college town. Sitting in a coffee shop in town, I observed the students and residents as they walked down the street. Many had their hair spiked, dyed in a variety of colors, wore skin-tight polyester-striped and polka-dot clothes, and tall shoes that must weigh about five pounds each. I took myself back to the time of Norman Rockwell, a well-known artist, most famous as a magazine illustrator. Part of his popularity came from using the Massachusetts town folk as his models for what I now know are "genre" paintings. In other words, he painted people in everyday settings doing ordinary things that take place in a small town: kids playing baseball, folks going fishing, people visiting the local doctor, or a young couple getting a marriage license, soldiers going off to war, a family saying the blessing over Thanksgiving dinner. With their portraits of ordinary American life in the first half of the twentieth century, his covers for the *Saturday Evening Post* and other popular magazines captured the spirit of Middle America .

Coincidentally, I had the privilege of meeting him when my family visited his Vermont home and studio in 1960. My mother-in-law said she would never wash her hands again after shaking his hand. So what would he think of, or more to the point, how would he portray the citizens of Northampton, Massachusetts, in 1995? I believe he would be astounded and amused and would once again give Americans the opportunity to see how our mores, fashions, and even our priorities have changed. Would he be tolerant? Would he be outraged? I rather think that after he asked, just as I would, "What is the world coming to?" he would attempt to talk to folks and find out they were much like at the people who walked these streets fifty years ago. Of course, they would have more sophisticated knowledge about the global situation, and he would likely be amazed by the widespread use of computers in this Information Age. But people's efforts to be noticed as individuals through what I see as their rather outrageous dress and shocking demeanor tells me that folks today have the same insecurities and eccentricities that they had in the '40s and '50s.

I experienced a number of humorous incidents while working in this setting. Of course, no matter where I work, I always find curiosity and snickering about my name. First of all, everyone thinks that "Jimmie" is a nickname—it is not. Then they snicker a bit at my last name, "Butts."

- I was suturing up a young Nigerian student one night. Since we had been quite busy, the young medical assistant working with me had already prepared the gentleman for my work. He had a laceration on his buttocks. I usually introduce myself to the patient before I administer any health care. In this case, I realized that I had not done so, and he was lying on his stomach and could not see my nametag. I told him that he would be quite amused when he learned my name. His wife looked at my nametag and laughed. At that, the patient asked, "What is so funny?" His wife told him that it had something to do with his injury. He guessed, "Is it Ms. Stitches?" He was amused, as we all were, when he learned that my last name was "Butts."

As in any urgent-care center, the work was feast or famine. Some nights would be quiet, and some would be unbelievably busy. And as usual, it was my last night on the assignment that kept me hopping all night. That night I saw twenty-four patients after midnight. Eight of them were intoxicated, and many had lacerations and broken bones. I suppose that, with the large number of people who utilize this facility, this is not uncommon. I worked with some great people and had a good experience in Northampton. As a matter of fact, I returned in 1996 to work a few day shifts in the clinic on my way to an assignment in Vermont. I have to say that daytime work was quite different and that if I went back, I would prefer the pace and practice of the midnight shift.

Talihina, Oklahoma

For two months, January and February 1996, I was assigned to Choctaw Nation Hospital in Talihina, Oklahoma. This part of the state is known as "Choctaw country," but it is not considered a reservation. This is where the majority of the Choctaw from Mississippi settled after they survived their Trail of Tears.

Angie Debo is the author of *The Choctaw Republic* and other books documenting events involving Native Americans. In 1970, she wrote *A History of the Indians of the United States*, in which she recounts the story of the "Trail of Tears." It began in 1830, when Andrew Jackson determined that Native Americans be moved west to less populated (and less desirable) areas. Most of the tribes were force-marched to Oklahoma, which had been set aside as an "Indian territory," the focus of the government's Indian policy through most of the nineteenth century. The liquidation of tribes and reservations began in 1887 and reached its peak in this state. In Oklahoma the move accomplished its goals of resettlement, dispersion of the people, and weakening the strength of these various tribes. Therefore, in many ways, the history of Oklahoma is a microcosm of the history of Native Americans since the arrival of Whites in the New World. By 1970, Oklahoma had the largest Indian population of any of the United States.

Talihina is a small town in the southeastern part of Oklahoma. In 1996, one thousand people lived there. As in many small towns across the country, there are signs of poverty or, let us say, economic deprivation. There are empty stores and little evidence of activity. The town is located off of a main highway, and after a Wal-Mart was built in Poteau, about seventy miles away, shoppers left town. I have witnessed this in many towns. I wonder if old Sam Walton knew what would happen to small businesses all across the country or if he or his heirs would care.

As usual, I visited the local cafés, the hardware store, craft shops, and the post office. When I go into grocery stores, I look and listen to people as they go about their daily activities. In Talihina, the decidedly Southern accents are familiar to me. Occasionally in the hospital, I heard some of the older natives speaking Choctaw, and of course, I did not understand a single word, though I did try to learn a few medical words in Choctaw so that I could communicate clearly with my patients.

The hospital was an old tuberculosis facility, built many years ago of native stone. I was impressed with its strength and the dignity that it must have had in its day. During my nurses training in Nashville, Tennessee, we were sent to the local county tuberculosis hospital for two weeks. When you visit one, you can expect the spirit of Florence Nightingale to be present to see that everything is in order and everyone is receiving good care. She was the first to teach that fresh air, good hygiene, and good nutrition are the essential elements of healing. This magnificent old building's old sun porches and well-ventilated halls are the remaining evidence of the days of the tuberculosis epidemic and the healing methods that were used to combat it.

In fact, it makes me seem a relic that I was in training before the discovery of INH and Streptomycin, the drugs that finally brought a halt to this epidemic. Tuberculosis is no respecter of persons, but there is still a high incidence in the Native American population. As I said before, when I was in Bethel, Alaska, most natives over the age of fifty had the scars of lung disease, as well as tuberculosis of the bone, kidney, and other, more serious infections.

The building and the grounds of the Choctaw Nation Hospital must have been quite attractive in the past, and for the most part, they have been well maintained. Like other hospitals in the United States, this hospital was experiencing downsizing. The outpatient clinics were busy every day. The Choctaw and other eligible patients come from at least one hundred miles away to have their hypertension, diabetes, and other chronic and acute illnesses treated. The pediatric clinic and the women's health clinic were busy, as well. The hospital also has a facility for abused mothers and their children, as well as an alcohol rehabilitation unit. Since my first assignment, the old hospital facility has been closed. You will read about the new hospital in Talihina when I return in 2000. Wow, what a difference that would prove to be!

I arrived in Fort Smith, Arkansas, in a huge snowstorm. In fact, I had left North Carolina in a snowstorm that dropped more white stuff there than we saw in Talihina. The snowflakes were big and fluffy and made Winding Stair Mountain look elegant and beautiful. As the snow melted during the next two days, all that was left was mud. I was reminded of my assignment in Bethel, Alaska: a small town, few inhabitants, and evidence of poverty. There are similar towns in North Carolina and all across the country. It made me think about those of us who live in modern, prosperous towns and cities, like Cary, North Carolina, who live rather extravagantly and may take for granted the beauty and wealth of their part of the country.

At the time of my assignment in Talihina, only ten hospital beds were open for new admissions. And this included the obstetrics ward and the nursery. I worked in the emergency room from 10:00 p.m. until 8:00 a.m. There were always a registered nurse and a practical nurse on site, and a doctor was on call for me if there was something that I could not handle. We were not very busy; some nights we would only see three or four people. However, if someone needed hospitalization for a serious condition, such as a heart problem or severe pneumonia, we had to "jump through all sorts of

84

hoops" to find a hospital that would admit a patient whose only insurance was provided by Indian Health.

We would be fairly busy from 10:00 p.m. until 2:00 a.m., seeing sick children, diabetics whose sugar was sky high, and others in hypertensive crises. There was a high incidence of respiratory disease, asthma, COPD (chronic obstructive pulmonary disease), and RSV (respiratory syntactical virus), which can be devastating for children under the age of two. When we were not busy seeing patients, we were asked to file massive numbers of charts of people who had been seen in the daytime clinics and in the emergency room. It seemed like a never-ending task.

I decided to write a humor column for *Choc-talk*, the hospital newsletter, and was later able to present my "Laugh for the Health of It" program for the entire hospital and clinic staff. The staff was quite discouraged about the hospital's financial situation, since they didn't know from one day to the next if they would be "downsized." In some ways, health care in the trenches is not different from the situation in the medical Meccas of the rest of the nation. The Choctaw chief at that time wanted to make all of the decisions about running the hospital. I learned that even though many of the natives had other insurance and Medicare or Medicaid, the secondary insurance plans were never billed. Doing so would not have been illegal, and it would have helped to defray the charges that were not covered by Indian Health Services.

Once again, I met the real heroes in a situation like this—the nurses, doctors, and staff members who stay in these areas. There were so many of us who came and went. Some of the caregivers were more skilled than others. My biggest fear was my lack of experience in cardiac care. The nurses were astute and up-to-date on the procedures that could be performed. I was assured that my consulting physician would come in when I needed him. One night, however, when I felt the patient needed more than I could provide, the consulting physician finally dragged himself in and asked for the book on ACLS (acute cardiac life skills), and I learned that before he took this assignment, he had done nothing but insurance physicals during his previous twenty years of practice. Thank God for the nurses.

As the snow melted and the temperature soared to 55 degrees, I was able to explore this rough land. Folks farm and raise cattle, but those seem like impossible tasks because the earth is covered with rocks. The terrain is almost impossible to hike on. The cows looked scrawny to me and were fed hay that was purchased and trucked in rather than grazing on lush pastures that I was accustomed to back East, especially in Vermont, where the cows were gigantic.

The rocks around Talihina appear to be a combination of sandstone and shale. There is probably some flint in the area, but I never identified any. I assumed this, since the Native Americans did use flint to make arrowheads. [Ed.—I believe most of the Native Americans' flint was imported from the Ozarks, the Wichita (or Washitah) Mountains, and from the Flint Hills of northeastern Kansas.]

On the rough terrain of these hills, nothing seems to grow except poison ivy and rough cedar trees. Remarkably, many cows graze these hills, and I guess they eat briars and thistles. There were also goats, sheep, chickens, and some farms that raised fighting cocks. I had never seen a chicken farm where each rooster had its own little shed to which he was tethered. The roosters have to be separated so they will not kill each other. Many farmers have a variety of livestock, and in the valleys or on plains, there are some healthy looking cows, some with very long horns, and Brahmas, as well as lots of horses, some of which are Morgans. It must be expensive to feed all of this livestock, but it appears to be quite common. Teenagers are very involved with the animals, and many of these children are active in the local 4-H clubs. Of course, I'm a city girl, so what do I know?

As I stood on the top of a hill, I could see the beauty of the valleys with many ponds (or "tanks," as they are called); amidst the trees, houses dotted the landscape, and the land appeared rich. Yet, on closer observation, there appeared to me to be a great deal of poverty. I could see shacks, old trailers, half-finished houses, some of which seemed to have been under construction for a number of years. Many yards were littered with broken-down vehicles, discarded appliances, and just plain trash. I saw the land as hostile to any kind of easy living.

Yet, by traveling in any direction, one encounters land that seems more attractive and forgiving. The valleys look more productive and peaceful. The trees still appear to be young, less than fifty years old. The area was logged to the bare dirt seventy years ago, and is being revived by Weyerhaeuser to support what will eventually become a substantial timber-harvesting industry.

While in Talihina, I took a number of excursions. The Gilcrease Museum in Tulsa has an extensive collection of art created by Native Americans and others who loved the scenes of this wild country. I was impressed by the carvings of Willard Stone, a native who had a severe injury to his right hand, yet still became a gifted sculptor. The native art is beautiful, and I showed great restraint in making purchases. I visited a place in Talihina called the "Redneck Corner" that offered crafts on consignment, but I decided that I preferred buying directly from the crafts' creators. A Choctaw woman named Betty Jack sent some lovely beadwork for me to see, and I succumbed to its charms, purchasing a lovely necklace that is the symbol of the Choctaw nation. While in Talihina, I purchased an angel ornament, a patch with the emblem of the Choctaw nation, and a book called *Ghosts of the Kiamichi Mountains*, written by a seventy-nine-year-old woman, Evelene Steele.

As in Alaska, the most beautiful sight I saw was the sky. The brilliant reds and purples one sees at sunset and the many stars in this vast sky at night are equally breathtaking. The scissortail is the state bird. I also was excited to see an actual roadrunner, and I knew that my children and grandchildren—who adore the antics of the cartoon Roadrunner as he constantly foils his pursuing enemy, Wile E. Coyote—would be delighted that I had now seen a real roadrunner. There were many hawks, and I saw a lone eagle over the Sardis Reservoir near the town of Heavener.

In Heavener, I went to see the "rune," a stone with an inscription that is believed by some to have been made by Vikings who traveled from Scandinavia and Greenland down the coast of North America until they found the Mississippi and Arkansas Rivers, eventually arriving in Oklahoma. I must admit that I found this hard to believe. There are about four other sites nearby where similar inscriptions were found, and these "runestones" are an interesting phenomenon. A local native herbalist was offended that anyone might suggest that Native Americans were not the true creators of such inscriptions. She felt that this implies that the Native Americans were not as "advanced" as the Vikings.

The patients I saw were are all Native Americans, mostly Choctaw. They showed a high incidence of diabetes, asthma, hypertension, and the problems that obesity brings. For me, the emergency room was mostly quiet after midnight. The most frustrating part of my experience was the difficulty of having no open beds in the hospital when a patient needed to be admitted, which meant that we would have to transfer the patient to another facility. It appeared that other facilities were simply reluctant to accept transfers from the Choctaw Native Hospital. At the time, I had trouble understanding their reluctance. Now I know that the reimbursement rate for admitting and treating a Native American patient was limited to what the Indian Health Service could pay, much like a Medicare reimbursement.

After a couple of weeks, I learned more about the history of Native Americans and the movement of so many from their original homelands to Oklahoma. Most of the Choctaw had come from Mississippi. They had traveled the "Trail of Tears" after being forced to leave by Andrew Jackson. Many others had come of their own accord. Because I was born in Tennessee and had lived near Andrew Jackson's home, I was disappointed by the role that Andrew Jackson had in this travesty.

There are actually thirty-seven tribes from all over the United States that are represented in Oklahoma. Some are very active in keeping the culture of their individual tribes alive and practicing the customs of the past. Others are very modern, and except for being registered as proof of having an Indian heritage, one would not know that they were Native Americans. It would be the same if those of us who claim to be Irish had to prove that a certain percentage of our heritage was actually Irish in order to become "card-carrying Irish" to receive special benefits.

Choctaw Nation Hospital is now run by the Choctaw tribe and not by Indian Health Services. In 1996, the hospital was struggling to remain viable. At that time, there was much sadness among the administration and staff over its financial state. The hospital's budget still depends on funds from the federal government, and with the budget cuts of 1995–6, it seemed inevitable that the hospital would not survive.

When I was tempted to wear my administrative hat, I would get all sorts of ideas about how the hospital could survive financially and continue to serve the community with quality, cost-effective care. Evidently, a consultant had been brought in, and as far as the nurses knew, the only solution offered by the consultant was to reduce the nursing staff, and in so doing, the way that nurses were notified of their dismissal sometimes seemed thoughtless, to say the least.

I am happy to say that by the time I returned to Talihina in January 2000, the Choctaw Nation had built a brand-new hospital; the entire situation—the building, the delivery of health care, and the treatment of the staff—had gone from abysmal to remarkable.

Lufkin, Texas

East Texas! Each community in our country has a personality of its own, as individual as the human beings who inhabit it. East Texas is no exception. Lufkin, located in Angelina County, is a town of thirty-four thousand people that maintains the warmth and amenities of Small Town, USA; yet has many modern conveniences, as well as big-city social and health problems. Of course, working in the Angelina County Health District, I had more opportunities to see, up close and personal, a large variety of problems.

The Angelina Health District serves the indigent people of Angelina County. The clinic serves a number of purposes, most of which are accomplished under the same roof. On any weekday morning, there was a crowd of people waiting for the doors to open at 8:00 a.m. The clinic's services include immunizations, STD (sexually transmitted disease) screening and treatment, prenatal and well-child care, financial screening, plus the services provided by the primary-care clinic and laboratory. Many of the patients speak only Spanish, and several of the employees are bilingual. Although I have attempted to learn this melodic language, my ears are just too slow to understand it as well as I should.

I flew into Shreveport, Louisiana, on a Saturday in early September 1996. There are a number of gambling casinos in this town, but I did not see much of it on my way to Texas. From there, my drive through what is called the "piney-woods" country was

Hispanic children at Lufkin Clinic in Lufkin, Texas (1996).

pleasant. My accommodations in Lufkin had been described as a "furnished apartment." This is usually more than adequate, but I learned that "furnished" does not necessarily include dishes, sheets, cooking equipment, etc. Therefore, it was Monday evening before I got approval to purchase the necessary items, all of which I found at the local Target store.

On September 7, I started my orientation. That first day, I saw most of the patients so that the departing nurse practitioner could catch up on some paperwork before she left to have her baby, which was due on September 20. Luckily for her, but not for me, she delivered on September 8, so that was the end of my orientation. The support staff was terrific. And despite my having to jump into the fray immediately, it was most interesting.

In Lufkin, I saw more pathology among the one hundred patients I examined and treated during my first week than most providers see in six months. The majority of diabetics I saw were Type II, with end-organ diseases ranging from retinopathy to kidney failure. There were many hypertensive patients whose "best" blood pressure readings were around 160/100 when we prefer readings of 135/85 or less. I saw fewer colds and sinus infections than in any other practice in which I had worked during the previous two years. Skin infections—such as impetigo; tinea and cellulitis—were frequent complaints. Inmates from the local jail were brought in if they needed medical attention, and there were two or three prisoners to be seen each day. I must admit that the local constabulary had excellent advice about the best places to eat and the best fishing holes.

As always, I want you to hear both the medical stories and the anecdotes that describe the local culture. First, I will tell the medical stories.

As I said before, the amount and variety of pathology I saw was phenomenal. Each day, I wished that there were a nurse-practitioner student to precept. That student would have witnessed, first hand, illnesses some providers have only read about in textbooks and will never actually see. Each day I saw a patient with the typical symptoms of adult-onset diabetes: extreme thirst, frequent urination, weight loss, weakness, and reduced libido. Most spoke no English, but the translators had dealt with this scenario often, and I began to spot these patients as soon as they came in the door. I also saw diabetics whose disease was so advanced that they could no longer control their blood sugar, even by taking their medications.

- I lamented over the plight of a fifty-one-year-old Hispanic woman who was having a difficult time controlling her blood sugar. In less than three weeks, I saw her three times for a variety of complaints that were basically somatic, ranging from dizziness to back pain, any or all of which may have been related to her diabetes or to her work or sleep habits or who knows what. I was frustrated about my inability to find a treatment that would help her feel better. Then, through the help of a translator, I learned more about her social history.

Three months before I saw her, two of her sons had been wounded in a drive-by shooting. A third young man, a friend of her sons, had been killed. Her third son had married a fourteen-year-old girl three years before, and they were proving to be a burden for my patient, living in her house and needing more help than they were contributing.

On the fourth visit, I felt helpless to do anything to alleviate her back pain; anti-inflammatory medicines had not helped, and no chiropractic care or physical therapy was available. I asked the translator to leave after I had explained my concerns to the patient. I positioned myself behind the patient so that I could give her a back massage for about five minutes. I rubbed her neck, shoulders, and upper back silently, since we spoke different languages. The value of this small gesture was made clear to me as she left, however, when she smiled and said, "Gracias." How nice it would have been if she could have received a similar respect and kindness at home.

- A forty-seven-year-old gentleman with a history of alcoholism and tobacco abuse (four packs of cigarettes a day) developed a blood clot in his left arm and had such serious peripheral vascular disease that he could not work. As we were preparing to do an electrocardiogram, I found that the EKG lead I placed on his left arm, where the clot had been removed, would only work when it was located below the antecubital area. Nurses who work in coronary care may have known that, but let's face it, when have I seen a patient with such a history?

- One day, a twenty-one-year-old woman from Mexico arrived with two prescriptions written in Spanish. I knew enough to realize that one was for 500 mg doses of Tetracycline, of which she was to take two pills twice a day. The other was for three doses of Penicillin G—1,200,000 mg each—to be administered intramuscularly, one every three weeks. She also handed me a laboratory report, written in Spanish, and I finally figured out that it gave the results of an ASO titer (a test to diagnose possible streptococcal infection), which were twice the normal value. Her husband then told me the woman's uncle was a doctor in Mexico who was treating for "fever in her bones." She had complained of pain in her joints and had a history of many sore throats as a child. I immediately thought, "*Rheumatic fever!*" Well, I didn't know that for sure. She had no heart murmur and no rash and seemed to be in no acute distress except for our mutual lack of understanding. Another local doctor had prescribed Synthroid for some reason, so I had another puzzle to put together. With this patient, I felt badly because I could not speak Spanish; this case, however, would have been tough even in English, since I didn't have her previous health records. I thought, "Where is that student who would learn so much from seeing this patient?" And more appropriately, "Where is the doctor that I can consult with during the day?" He only stopped by once a week to sign more than one hundred of my charts in fifteen minutes. He was helpful when I pinned him down, but he was overworked in his private practice and not always available to me. I saw the patient for her third injection, and I am still hoping for her recovery.

These issues brought to my mind another subject that deserved some thought. In 1996 as the healthcare crisis seemed to be escalating despite the attempts to have more "gatekeepers" in the form of HMOs (health maintenance organizations) and federal, state, and county regulations designed to control costs. I was even more concerned about the *quality* of care.

As a family nurse practitioner with twenty years experience, I felt I was a fairly decent provider with a good sense of my skills, knowledge, and limitations. Ah, yes, my limitations! As I presented some very complicated cases to the consulting physician, he told me that all I needed was a little more "confidence." Perhaps. But what I really needed in this setting was an experienced physician. I know that this statement might agitate some of my fellow nurse practitioners, who would contend that most nurse practitioners are competent to handle almost every patient who comes into a primary care center. I have never pretended to know as much as our physician colleagues know, or to trust in my own good judgment and skills to the point of believing that I could handle every case without a sound relationship with a competent physician. I know that many of my colleagues are exceptionally competent, knowledgeable, and confident in many highly specialized practices. But I still contend that a sound relationship with the attending physician is basic. I want to be a nurse, not a doctor. A nurse has some skills that most doctors just do not possess. Even doctors who have the compassion and empathy that are necessary supplements to the healing arts, must spend much of their time keeping their education and diagnostic skills up to date, not to mention learning more about the treatment of complicated illnesses. I personally think that it would be dangerous if a nurse practitioner's "confidence" turned into cockiness and he or she were tempted to take on more responsibility than would be considered medically sound.

I must admit that I have enjoyed taking on the challenges these patients brought to me. Perhaps I would not have learned as much if the responsibility had not been thrust upon me. This is probably one of the reasons that I continued to accept these assignments in remote places with limited resources—to test myself, to see just how much I could do. If I have learned nothing else, I have learned the truth of my old adage, proven to me over and over each day: *"Caring is just as valuable as curing."* Most of the time, caring just takes a little more time than the usual fifteen-minute appointment slot. In the final analysis, I believe in the team concept: a doctor and a nurse practitioner teamed up can give the best of their individual talents to the patient. And I am still an idealist.

As the weeks passed, I did feel a bit more confident and relaxed about accepting realistic limits on my desire to "cure" folks—that is, to heal them, which I could not always do—realizing that the best that I could do on most days was to provide them with adequate caring. Lufkin was the most challenging place I've worked, and the pathology there was almost overwhelming. Of course, I saw folks who returned for follow up visits, and I felt more productive. When I work in emergency rooms, I rarely get to see the patients again or find out if their condition truly improved or became worse as a result of my diagnosis and treatment.

I also had some time to review some of the medical records and get a feeling for how some of these folks had been diagnosed and treated by the various providers who had preceded me. One doctor who had worked in the clinic used a colorful vocabulary in his notes. He had written an interesting letter to the Texas Disability Department about a patient seeking a declaration of disability, which would qualify the patient to receive services. The doctor gave an eloquent explanation of all of the reasons that the gentleman should be declared disabled, yet ended it by stating that, despite all the patient's needs, the state of Texas had denied the disability claim by using the "east Texas philosophy… if it walks like a duck, then it must be a duck!!!" which implied the Disability Department believed that if the man could walk at all, he surely was not disabled.

There is a mystery here about who is eligible to receive disability. The medical care in the United States may be the best in the world, but the administrative paperwork is a nightmare, and that is where much of the blame for the high cost of medical care truly resides. Contrary to my strong belief in the current structure of our healthcare system, I am more and more inclined to think that a one-party-payer system deserves some serious consideration.

More about East Texas

During my time in Lufkin, I was able to take part in a variety of leisure activities. Many people there are avid fishermen and fisher women. I have always heard that folks will never reveal their most productive fishing holes. A friend and I went to the Attoyak River, where a large catfish was rumored to have been caught that very morning. Under a bridge, we climbed down the bank of a typical east Texas river, which was then about thirty feet wide, as opposed to its width of several hundred feet in the flood condition, and I got stuck in the mud of its floodplain. It felt as if I were walking in quicksand. I was terrified and called for my friend to rescue me, which he did in short order. When we first arrived, we had noticed that the current was swift and that herons were hovering nearby, so we thought we might get lucky and catch a fish. But all I got was muddy feet and a jolt of fear when I thought I was sinking into a pit of quicksand. Giving up on catching any catfish, we drove over the Sabine River into Louisiana on Highway 21 to eat catfish at a restaurant. It turned out to be delicious, since we didn't have to catch it.

In October, some of us went to Tyler, Texas to the famous Rose Festival. The roses were exceedingly beautiful, and any rose that started to look wilted was doomed to the shears; the gardeners had groomed them to perfection. The aroma was exquisite. We saw part of the Rose Festival parade, including the Queen as she rode near the end of the procession. The atmosphere was like Mardi Gras in

New Orleans, but without people wandering the streets drinking "hurricanes" and other alcoholic beverages in public. In New Orleans, the "hurricane" is the favorite alcoholic concoction of French Quarter tourists, and walking around the streets with alcohol is permissible!

Driving back to Lufkin, we stopped at the Caddoan Mounds, where the Caddo tribes had inhabited the grasslands many centuries before. There we visited the small museum and attended a Native American festival. Unfortunately, there were no Caddos in attendance, since they are almost extinct.

I went to a Stephen F Austin University football game in Nacogdoches that was fun to watch. There was also a local playhouse in Lufkin, and I got to see *Driving Miss Daisy* and, on another occasion, a Neil Simon play.

All in all, it was a satisfactory assignment, and I would go back if they asked me.

One event that occurred there changed my life. Right before coming home, I found a breast lump under my left nipple. In the next chapter, I will share with you the emotional experience and physical treatment of, as well as my recovery from breast cancer.

"We interrupt this program…"

When I started this book, I had decided not to refer to my breast cancer. Yet, my experience with this dread disease did slow me down and gave me new insights into health care. And friends encouraged me to share the experience of my breast cancer with you, my readers.

I have been one of the lucky ones. After discovering a lump in my breast near the end of my assignment in Lufkin, Texas, I wrote in my journal, first on December 16, when my physician called to give me the bad news, and later on Christmas Day to express my reaction to this new challenge in my life. When Dr. Yarborough, my surgeon and friend, called me, I could tell by his voice that he was sad to give me the report of my biopsy. It was as if someone had said, "We interrupt this program to bring you a special announcement: you have *cancer*!" My fears of learning the status of a cancer in my body for the third time in my life (having had, as I have mentioned, thyroid cancer with subsequent surgery on three occasions) and of having to make decisions about treatment seemed insurmountable. These reflections are my attempt to express my fears and hopes at that time:

Reflections: December 16, 1996

For almost a year I worked on a little book called *The Humor Factor*. For a number of years, I have written and still write a column by that name for the *North Carolina*

Nurse Practitioner Newsletter. I wanted to collect those columns and other stories from my life and career in a little book. I decided to self-publish it because I cannot stand rejection. I worked with a local printer, and today, two thousand books arrived at my home. I was so excited. It turned out pretty well for my first attempt at a book.

While opening the boxes and looking at the final result, I received a phone call. It was my friend and surgeon with bad news. He was quite upset to tell me that the biopsy on my breast proved the lump to be malignant. We both cried a little, and later I cried a lot. Why now, when I am on my great adventure must I interrupt my life to deal with breast cancer? Yes, I found the lump under my left nipple. It was rubbery, irregular and tender. My mammogram was negative. The biopsy seemed insignificant. What do most women do who get this news? They cry or throw things, make important decisions about the treatment options, and figure how to continue their lifestyles while moving forward. My sister, Joy, has had two occurrences of breast cancer, five years apart, the latter more than twenty years ago, and she is still alive. The surgical techniques in use then left her with many scars and bitterness over the loss of her breasts and her physician husband, who left her after her surgery. That frequently happens when a woman loses her breast.

I was more fortunate. To those who truly loved me, the eventual loss of my breasts made no difference in their love and devotion. I am the one who misses that part of my body. It has been more than five years, and I am alive and well. Each time an ailment occurs in my body, however, I feel a certain amount of fear and trepidation about a recurrence. But I got on with my life with few changes in my goals.

Christmas Day, 1996

Reflections written over the past three or four years seemed to come easy. Today, I write with hesitancy. I am filled with gratitude for the wonderful gifts that I have received over the sixty-one-plus years of my life. I rejoice in the gifts of a good husband, a life free of any material needs that could not be met, the births of three wonderful children, and a lovely place in which to live, worship, and work.

This month I received a gift in a strange package. I have just learned that I have breast cancer. Sounds terrible, doesn't it? So many times I have been with family, friends, and patients, and shared this terrible news with them and tried to say the right things and behave in the best way to offer comfort and sometimes guidance. I am not sure that we ever say or do the right things.

I have a number of thoughts that I would like to explore. When Norma Jean [an aunt we all loved] was alive, she told me so many times that—despite the fact that she had debilitating arthritis, and liver disease, and died of an aneurysm at age sixty-nine—she just prayed that she would never have *cancer*. When Gayle Pezzoni [mother-in-law of my daughter, Becky] died, she was incapacitated for so many months without being able to communicate her feelings, as I do at this moment. We did not even know if she was aware of anything that was taking place around her. Mom [my mother-in-law], with all of her ailments, seemed to wish for her life to end, as she seemed depressed at the loss of her loved ones and less contact with her family and less independence. Then Joy Odom, [a young neighbor, teacher, and friend] had the most mysterious illness of them all, taking her away from her young family at what should have been the prime time of her life.

I am the lucky one. I know (perhaps too much) the things that I will or may have to deal with over the next few months. The worst part of being a nurse is that we look at the worst possibilities. I have no real idea that I will have to be treated with chemotherapy or radiation, yet as I fussed with my hair this morning, I was thankful that I still have hair. Who knows if I will have any to fuss over this time next year? (I do have an ugly skull, with dents and irregularities from birth trauma, etc.) I look in the mirror and see an imperfect, scarred body, and cannot imagine what in the world I will see in a few weeks and wonder how in the world I will dress to be as attractive as I can be. Sounds terribly vain, yet I am not foolish enough to deny that in this time and in this place, there is a value placed on physical appearance.

I do not want to sound dramatic or even frivolous, but I feel I must speak what is in my mind. I know in my heart that it is not the physical appearance that makes the person. It seems that when we must face the person behind the face and body, that the challenge is to know who the real person is under that covering and preserving whatever is there that is good and right. Perhaps I fear that, underneath it all, I am really not a good or decent person worthy of the love of those who have rallied around with their thoughts and prayers. Oh, yes, without our clothes and a little makeup, there is a very vulnerable person inside. My friends and family have expressed a variety of responses to this news. They all pray so well. They seem to have a direct line to God. Of course, each one who has faced tragedy, fear and loneliness has developed a very personal relationship with our God.

Personally, I have avoided daily contact with my Maker. My excuses are that I don't want to bother Him with petty needs, when in reality I usually do not feel worthy to talk to Him daily as I did when I was younger. I have a few sins that I enjoy and do not want to abandon. I am sure that He knows every one and must be shaking His head as I go about doing the things that I want to do, even if those things happen to help a few needy people on the way.

Most of my confusion today has to do with whether or not I have been a decent mother and grandmother. No mother could have loved her children more, yet I feel that my responsibility for them ended when they reached adulthood. I have a career and a desire to explore new adventures and continue to provide nursing in needy places.

I will not lie and say that I have no fear about the illness. I do. Those fears have to do with more than the change in my appearance. They have to do with pain, nausea, and disability (or at least less stamina and flexibility); a larger fear is to think about the stage of the "invasive carcinoma" from my breast to other parts of my body and what that will mean, not so much in terms of facing the possibility of death as for how it will affect my lifestyle.

I have often thought that death by heart attack was my preference; then I would not have to think about all of these things. Yet I must not be finished with whatever it is that God has for me to do on this earth, so I must be on the lookout for what to do with this new "gift" in a very strange package. Is it to test if good humor and a positive attitude will make a difference? Will those who have yet to face such a dilemma benefit or learn from my experience? At the moment, learning and searching for meaning is the approach that I am taking.

Carl [my husband] says that he is pragmatic about the whole issue. Webster says that to be "pragmatic" is to be "busy, active, practical... pragmatism is a quality or condition of being a pragmatic, a system of philosophy which tests the validity of all concepts by their natural results." I am not so sure that is what he believes. It seems that to him being pragmatic means that we accept this challenge and go about the business of our lives, dealing with the reality of what must be done to handle the situation. I think this is what he believes, and I choose his definition over Mr. Webster's.

Whatever it means, I do recognize that Carl will be there with me through this entire ordeal. Unfortunately many who have this to face do not have the good fortune to have such a partner and helpmate. I am grateful for this gift. I have loved him for many years and even that love has undergone changes just as we have. I am grateful for his loyalty.

I am also grateful to those who may be less pragmatic, those who grieve, complain, and give me permission to do the same. Despite my quest to approach all facets of life positively, putting on a happy face and remembering to look for the humor in all things, they say that it is okay to cry, to be angry and afraid, and to say so. Yes, I need that kind of love, sympathy, and permission, as well. I am grateful for this gift.

Well, it is Christmas Day and a time for gifts. As I said, my gift has come in a strange package. There is much to endure and many decisions to be made over the next few weeks. I pray that as I take the wrappings off, discover the truth of what I must face and deal appropriately with all of the implications, I will be brave, afraid, angry, and loving. I want to say and do what is best for my kids. I am sorry that our genetic history is so strong for cancer, asthma, and heart disease. Carl is so much healthier than I am (yet I feel healthy, despite all I have had to deal with, this being my third bout with cancer.) Perhaps the kids and grandkids will carry his gene more than mine.

For me, the things that I will need in order to face this challenge will be forthcoming: the most caring medical treatment that one could ever ask for, the support of many friends and family members, and the opportunity to make amends for whatever I may have done that has been harmful. What more could I ask? I pray that all of these family members love one another and are there for one another now and in the future… Birth order, individual personalities, all that psychological stuff aside, I rejoiced with each birth experience, each infant who I rocked and attempted to sing lullabies and melodies to as I held them in my arms, just as I have with each grandchild. I swell with pride when they are successful in their work and in their play. As they get older, they seem to realize that success doesn't always have to do with materialism. Yet they are in the age of materialism, just as we were at that age. Only experience and age will teach them the true wealth in our lives on this earth. I am just beginning to learn that myself.

Wealth for me now has to do with the true love, intimacy, sharing, and exploring ideas with individuals whom I have known for years. These people are those whom I have met in my career, past and present. Wealth has to do with seeing those I love delight in a starry sky, a sunrise or sunset, and in doing things for one another. I don't mean big things. I mean showing kindness, consideration, and tolerance for the similarities and differences that those of us in a family just have. Words like patience, nurturing, and learning together mean as much as the laughter. I know that I am loved. If there is one lesson I would want to share, it is that love is like a boomerang: it always comes back to you. You cannot give it away. It does not have a price on it. It teaches us how to respect one another despite our differences. And it trickles down into our children and will extend to their friends and their children. Conflict acts like a dam that stops that love from taking its natural course.

Carl said that it is okay to be angry, but to stay angry does no good. I have learned how to express anger better than I used to. I used to just cry and be depressed. Now I am sometimes perceived as arrogant, and I regret that. It is just that I am still learning to express myself over my impatience with my own inadequacies. There are a number of things that I enjoy now that help me to deal with anger: learning—learning more about my profession; learning to hear music I never listened to before; learning about philosophy and anthropology and what makes people tick; allowing myself to feel the fears and passions that most of us stuff away or express in inappropriate ways; writing, which gives me an opportunity to explore my emotions and my reactions to the challenges and joys of each day; and there is more that I want to do. I want to paint pictures, create; be well enough to take long walks; spend more time, quiet time with each family member, yes, one at a time, so that I can really listen to what each has to say.

Yes, I have received a gift, an illness that will not take away the opportunity to finish doing some of the things that I want to do. For that I am extremely grateful. I was once told that despite having many "friends," most people usually have fewer than five who are true friends. These are the ones that you can pour out your heart and soul to and not fear repercussions. You can have different opinions, different beliefs, yet you can trust that friend to listen, respond, and gain more understanding about life, the world and even the universe. It seems easier to do this with friends than with family members. I find that to be very sad. How, oh Lord, can I approach this illness?

On the day in which we remember the greatest gift of love, the first gift, the gift of your Son, I am reflective, afraid, and yet grateful for the opportunity or challenge that I now face. I pray that I can discover the path that I must take to fully respond to this gift. Give me strength, wisdom, courage. You have already given me love, so much that it just spills out, though it is not always expressed in appropriate ways. Again, take me, make me, mold me, fill me so that I may fulfill your purpose for my life.

I believe, despite what I believed as a child, that illness is not happening to me because I have not been a good person. Otherwise Jean, Ann, Marie, Joy, and all of those wonderful people who have become ill recently would not have become ill. I also believe that You are indeed trying to direct my attention to some unfinished business. If be Thy will, please let me continue to love all those I love in many places and in many ways. Bless each of them as they seek to understand the mysteries of our complex lifestyles, our inequities, our materialism, our health challenges and the mysteries of one another's faith. Help me to understand why there must be so much chaos, animosity, selfishness, and lack of peace in our homes, our nation, and in the world. Tell me what to do. I will try to listen attentively and respond appropriately. I am only human, so continue to be patient with me.

Ultimately, I decided to have a simultaneous bilateral mastectomy and reconstructive surgery, which were performed in January 1997. I was not prepared, however, for the painful and difficult recovery.

In April 1997, I walked onto a stage at North Carolina State University to give a speech about courageous women who had made history in this country. I was uncertain and apprehensive that I could do it. I had never cancelled a speaking engagement in all my years as a public speaker. It turned out to be the best speech that I have ever given. The audience was sensitive to my slow movements. They seemed to appreciate my willingness to take the podium and share the enthusiasm that women should celebrate for their accomplishments during the past two centuries. They laughed appropriately when I was humorous. They cried when I spoke about the trials of women in our history. And I received a standing ovation.

I do not like to talk about my experience with cancer. I think it is because I am one of the lucky people who are alive and well. I have lost many patients and many friends and loved ones who were not so lucky. But you need to know that life goes on and you can still reach out to catch the brass ring and spread the gift of caring to everyone you know. If nothing else, my appreciation for each day's succulent gifts is keen. Consider the challenges and the opportunities that you face each day. Go for it!

Upon learning of my breast cancer, I became reflective and prayerful. My life was interrupted for a few months and periodically over the next five years, but I have been blessed and continued to travel, work, write, and live life to the fullest. Now I will continue with the next of my adventures working in the trenches of health care.

Back in North Carolina

Since my "retirement" in March of 1994, I have been away from home a lot, but I have loved the sights I have seen, as well as the varied cultures and healthcare settings I have encountered. Somehow, I have managed to be at home for most holidays and birthdays. Moreover, I found that there are those who needed help in primary care settings in Cary and in Raleigh. So I began to do contract work for a number of healthcare providers: the Health Care Center at SAS Institute (from which I had retired), Crosby Center Pediatric Clinic in inner-city Raleigh, with the Wake County Public Health Department offering care for poor families, and with a private practice in Cary called MacGregor Physicians.

The value of discussing these settings is to think about the more typical health care with which most of us are familiar, rather than that provided in the less prosperous places where I had worked in 1994 and 1995.

Returning to SAS Institute, a highly successful software-development company, reminded me of how fortunate its employees and their families are. They come to the Health Care Center, located on site, and are seen by a nurse practitioner, physician, physical therapist, psychologist, or nutritionist, depending on their needs. They can have immunizations (routine or travel related), receive the services of a nurse for blood pressure checks, and have laboratory tests performed at the request of private physicians or on-site providers.

The convenience is phenomenal, and they pay no fees for these services. Family members can be covered for these services for very reasonable monthly fees.

If they choose to seek medical services elsewhere, there are no limits on which medical provider they choose to see in the community in order to have insurance cover a large portion of the medical costs, including physical examinations, diagnostic radiology tests, and prescription drugs.

This concept of on-site health care has been so successful that many other companies, legislatures, and health maintenance organizations have sought to learn just how it works. And the SAS Institute experience has been written and spoken about in many medical journals and nursing schools across the country. I am happy that I was fortunate to have been the first one hired to institute this model of health care, and have been astounded to see how it has continued to grow and operate while delivering tremendous healthcare cost savings to SAS Institute.

I felt, and still feel, an array of emotions when returning to SAS Institute. Despite the success of the program started in 1984 by me with the support of David Russo, Director of Human Resources; Jim Goodnight, CEO of SAS Institute; and John Sall, Vice President, I do not regret retiring from that position at the age of fifty-nine. As the Health Care Center grew and the staff grew to twenty-two people, I was seeing fewer and fewer patients. Management became the biggest part of my responsibilities. After much thought and deliberation about working in the field of nursing and what it meant to me, I realized that I could give up that prestigious position to pursue my desire to provide hands-on care to people in a variety of settings.

Today there are more than fifty-five employees in the Health Care Center, and they have opened an additional clinic to serve more than ten thousand people. Am I envious? Do I have regrets?

No, running an operation of that size is a management challenge that I would prefer to leave to someone else, someone who would enjoy performing the task. One of my emotions has to do with how I feel when I see the people who worked there with me. Then, the center was small, only one thousand square feet, and everyone on the staff saw each other every day. There was warmth and lots of good times in such a setting. We worked hard, and I experienced a camaraderie that was the best of my entire career.

Another emotion I felt on returning to North Carolina has to do with the vast difference between healthcare delivery in this metropolitan area of North Carolina and healthcare delivery in the areas where I have worked since the spring of 1994. The resources for patients in North Carolina are virtually unlimited, even for those who may be poor and uninsured.

The Cosby Center Pediatric Clinic was established to serve children who may or may not have Medicaid coverage. There was a full time pediatrician there as well as a nurse, social worker, and support staff. The receptionist knew the inner-city Raleigh neighborhood and was successful in bringing patients and their families into the center for quality care. Dr. Anne McLaurin, with whom I had worked prior to joining SAS Institute, also worked at the Crosby Clinic as an enthusiastic volunteer. Her ability to speak Spanish was important because some of the client families were from Mexico, having moved to Raleigh in search of work and educational opportunities. While working with indigent families all across the country, I have witnessed the appreciation that they have for dedicated healthcare workers. When a patient at the Crosby Clinic needed specialized services, we could refer that patient to a number of larger agencies, hospitals and specialty clinics. Unlike what I had experienced while working for Indian Health Services, it did not seem to take as long to accomplish such a feat. While in Bethel, Alaska, I had learned that referring a patient to Anchorage to see a specialist could take from six to twelve weeks. This was not the case in Raleigh, North Carolina.

MacGregor Family Practice is a busy private practice with a terrific staff. While working there, however, I had a rude awakening when I learned the real effect HMOs can have on a private practice. For each patient we saw, it was imperative to know who the insurance carrier was. Each HMO or insurance carrier specified which services would be reimbursed; what agencies, laboratories, diagnostic centers for radiology, ultrasound, etc., would be acceptable; and what specialists or hospitals were designated as options for the patient. Times were rapidly changing with the emergence of HMOs. Although the concept seemed cost effective originally, the hoops through which a patient or provider must jump and the limits on what services were reimbursable created a nightmare for private practices. Therefore, they select which patients they will care for depending on how many different agencies they must deal with.

To illustrate the challenge at MacGregor, I will tell you the story of a young mother whom I saw one day at four o'clock in the afternoon. She had lower-left quadrant pain and an elevated white blood-cell count. Since the patient history and physical examination did not fit a diagnosis of appendicitis, I decided that she needed an ultrasound and possible referral to a surgeon. A hospital is located within two miles of the office, and it seemed logical to me to send her there for her ultrasound. I learned, however, that her insurance would only cover the test if it were performed in a hospital that is within eighteen miles of the office. She had two young children who were coming home from school that afternoon. Because she could not locate her husband, she went home to see to the children herself and get them settled before going for her test. I had referred her to the nearby hospital before I knew the limits of her insurance. By the time I located her, she had gone to the first hospital, where I had to leave a message that she must go across town to have the test done and, if necessary, to see the surgeon or gynecologist that her HMO chose for her. She was eventually cared for, but I was extremely frustrated with the confusion over where to send her and to whom. This is the kind of situation that may discourage many of our healthcare employees from staying in the field.

Another example involves what I thought would be a simple treatment for toenails infected with a fungus. I could see clearly that the man suffering this infection needed one of the new oral medications that could quickly and effectively treat his condition. His insurance company, however, required that the fungus had to be cultured and sent to their chosen laboratory. If the culture tested positive, then they would authorize payment for liver studies that were to be performed prior to treatment. To treat the condition, they would only pay either for a specific prescription that was a few dollars cheaper than the new oral medication or for an older drug that was even less expensive but would take up to a year to cure the fungal infection. They wouldn't pay for the new drug that would take between six and twelve weeks to alleviate his condition.

You can see that what I thought was a travesty in Indian Health Services has now spread throughout private practice in the United States. Access to health care is now limited for all of us, depending on our insurer, whether private coverage, an HMO, Medicaid, or Medicare. With Americans' healthcare options becoming more and more limited, I began to understand why physicians were retiring at ever-younger ages and why the possibility of a single-payer system (socialized medicine) looks more attractive than ever before. It is common now that a Medicare patient who is not already under the care of a physician cannot find a caregiver who will accept a new Medicare patient, much less a Medicaid patient. After serving two years (1983–84) on a legislative committee to study why healthcare costs continue to escalate, I have only seen the situation become more complicated and cumbersome. You would think that a family practice would be eager to expand by accepting new patients and reaching out to the needy. In the larger cities, this does not seem to be the case. Wading through the mountain of forms, paperwork, and reimbursement limits is too costly for most practices. So physicians are retiring earlier or are changing or limiting their clientele.

There is a well-known joke about HMOs. It seems that three men went to heaven. As Saint Peter welcomed them, he asked each a question: "What did you do on earth to justify your admission into Heaven?" The first answered, "I was a doctor and cared for people for many years." St. Peter replied, "Well done; you may enter." The second replied, "I was a hospital administrator and managed a successful community service that provided quality care to all who came." At this response, St. Peter stroked his beard a little and then said, "Very well; you may enter." The third man replied, "I was the administrator of an HMO." After hesitating for several seconds, St. Peter told him. "Very well, you may enter these gates into Heaven, but you can only stay for three days."

I was soon eager to return to assignments in distant places once again. After a short assignment in Rocky Mount, North Carolina, during the summer, I was fortunate to have an assignment in Vermont, following a week in Amherst, Massachusetts, in the Student Health Clinic in September when the students were returning to school. The clinic was quite different from the Urgent Care Center at night, and I was glad to move to Vermont and the lovely Berkshire mountains in the fall.

Rutland, Vermont

After working for a while in North Carolina in 1997, I was on the road again. Fall in Vermont is gorgeous. The brilliant red and orange of the leaves against the white birch bark and the majestic evergreen trees on a sunlit day will take your breath away. In the fall of 1960, my family lived in Pittsfield, Massachusetts, near the Berkshire Mountains. That year this breathtaking season lasted about three days. The colors came with a cold wind, survived for a couple of days, and then it was over, blown away by colder winds that were quickly followed by a beautiful snow. I hoped for a longer season on this new assignment.

My job was in a family practice clinic owned by an HMO. The clinic had four physicians and a strong support staff of nurses, laboratory and radiology technicians, social workers, and office personnel. The plan was to hire a full time nurse practitioner, and I was to work until that person arrived. The physicians had privileges at the local hospital and were quite busy. To justify my presence for the next two months, the practice had expanded by taking on two thousand Medicaid patients.

They expected that these new patients would arrive with many health problems and that the nurse practitioner would see most of them and care for each of them in a fifteen-minute time slot. Needless to say, that was almost impossible. To see a new patient who was suffering from hypertension, diabetes, or other chronic disease; was taking a number of prescriptions; and had complications, both social and medical, was a huge challenge not only for me, but also for their whole operation.

The doctors were supportive and helpful to me, despite the fact that they were also seeing a large patient load from the already established practice. Of course, the long days also took a toll on my still-recovering body. But I soon realized that there was a better way to integrate this population into the current practice. Since most of the Medicaid patients had a number of illnesses, it was important that I learn as much about each patient as I could. My style is not to gather a laundry list of medicines they are taking. It is to find out where they live, who lives with them, whether or not they are working, how many children they take care of, what they fear about their health, their fears and hopes about life in general, and how they came to be on Medicaid. Many of these patients are "children having children," and in some cases, it seems to be a family tradition to get aid from the government. The impact of Medicaid on their lives can be significant; it can mean receiving good medical and obstetric care, access to birth control or abortion, or even more financial assistance if a mother does not marry her child's father. But, as you may surmise, I cannot do a decent job of this in a single fifteen-to-thirty minute visit.

I walked in to see one of the new patients; she was frantically drinking water, then excusing herself to go to the bathroom, passing water all the time, and I learned that despite eating voraciously, she was losing weight. This was a very typical new diabetic patient. She had what we call the "polys": polyuria (urinating a lot), ploydipsia (drinking a lot of water), and polyphagia (hungry all the time and eating a lot), yet she was losing weight. Granted, she was obese to begin with, so losing weight would not be a bad thing in itself, but it was happening for all the wrong reasons. Other common complaints from diabetics include things like "a little blurred vision," "no longer having orgasms," or as some southern men tell me, "I'm having a little trouble with my nature!" meaning problems with getting or maintaining an erection. Sometimes, they complain of a little dizziness or weakness. With the near epidemic of Type II diabetes in the United States today, it is time to do something drastic about obesity and its cause, Americans' fast-food, couch-potato lifestyle.

In the old days (as when my grandchildren ask, "What was it like in the olden days, Mimi?), a newly diabetic patient would be admitted to the hospital for extensive blood work, to see how much damage had already occurred to the kidneys, heart, or other major organs. Insulin would be started, and a teaching nurse would review each aspect of using insulin with the patient, a nutritionist would review the diabetic diet with the patient, and the hospital stay would last about three days, minimum. Now all of these steps have to be done on an outpatient basis, and because they are essential to the patient's survival, most of them have to be done on the first visit, depending on the level of the patient's blood sugar and whether or not sugar is being spilled in the urine.

So here I am with a new patient for a fifteen-minute visit. You can see my dilemma. I asked for some time to meet with my consulting physician, who had never worked with nurse practitioners before. I explained that if I could have forty-five to sixty minutes with each of these new patients, it would save the physicians a lot of time and distress in the long term. He agreed, and what a difference it made! Over the next two weeks, I had diagnosed other diabetics, not to mention congestive heart failure in hypertensive patients who had

Dr. Michael Garcia in Vermont (1997).

never understood how their medicine was supposed to work and were not taking the drugs properly, which resulted in frequent emergency room visits and hospitalizations. You can probably see where I am going. The "art of nursing" is truly more important than ever in both primary-care settings, where patients are first seen, and in high-tech hospitals, where nurses serve long hours and have a ton of paperwork to do. My second point is that it is up to those of us in primary-care nursing to empower patients with knowledge and understanding so that they can take the responsibility of caring for themselves and know when they are in trouble.

Now for a couple of patient stories:

- A forty-five-year-old gentleman came in complaining of ear pain. He was a Medicaid patient, living in a shelter in town. He did not appear to have had a bath in many days (or even weeks). He was toothless and looked much older than his actual age. His ears were completely blocked with hard wax. I could not budge the wax with my instruments. I filled his ears with a combination of oil and hydrogen peroxide to soften the wax; tried again, unsuccessfully, to remove it; and sent him back to the shelter with a supply of the drops. I asked him to put a few drops in each ear every night for a week and then to stand under a warm shower with his ears turned up to the stream of water. When he returned a week later, I hardly recognized him. He was so clean, smelled good, and had put in his false teeth. I was able to remove the remaining cerumen (wax) from his ears without difficulty. There was no infection, and he was delighted that he could hear so well. I was delighted that he had cleaned up so well!
- A seventy-eight-year-old woman came in with shortness of breath. She had hypertension and was on medications to control her blood pressure, which was not too elevated. Her ankles were swollen, and she had a very irregular heart beat.

It so happened that she was in severe congestive heart failure. I referred her to Dr. Garcia, who admitted her to the local hospital, and she eventually had successful surgery to correct a problem with her mitral valve. My physician seemed surprised that I had identified this problem.

It was interesting to me that in this small clinic, cancer patients could come in and receive chemotherapy for various cancers. One of the nurses had been trained to perform the chemotherapy procedures under protocols developed by the oncologists, who were near by. After working in Boston, I had the notion that all chemotherapy had to happen in major cancer centers.

Social Life in Vermont

The fall of September and October 1997 lasted a little longer than the three-day New England fall I remember from 1960. Rutland is very near to Lake Champlain, the Green Mountains, and other historic and scenic locations. Vermonters celebrate Halloween as much as the rest of the country celebrates Christmas. Decorations were everywhere. Every self-respecting house sported a makeshift graveyard with appropriate tombstones, ghosts, and ghouls. Pumpkins, haystacks, and gourds decorated every porch and yard. Store windows were adorned with black, gold, and orange in every display.

Every Sunday night, in every small town, many of the local churches held a "supper" for all comers, and for a small price, you could stuff yourself with delectable food and enjoy the fellowship of the residents. There were many craft and art shows where you could shop and buy to your heart's content. Since the winters are long, many artisans had finely honed their weaving, woodworking, and painting skills. Celebrating the harvest time included selling tasty apple dishes, as well as the maple syrup that we enjoy all over the country. Most of the farms are old, and the homes speak of the nature of the sturdy people who settled in this land.

The town of Rutland has accomplished a feat that many cities and town have not been able to. Downtown is vital. The quaint shops, stores, and cafés appear to be successful. I believe part of the success is due to the town requiring Wal-Mart to place its store and huge parking lot right in the center of town! This allows the shopper to kill two birds with one stone, discount shopping and yet still giving their other business to the local establishments. Having all of these amenities within walking distance gives an advantage to all.

One of my most favorite excursions was to go to Lake Champlain for a late supper one evening. That night, I looked up to the sky and saw a wondrous light that seemed to be dancing. At first, I thought it must be an auto dealership casting a spotlight into the cloudy fall sky to advertise a sale. Then I realized I was far away from any car dealership. It was the *Northern Lights*! What a show! The blue, purple, and pink ribbons undulating across the sky were breathtaking. Many times in my dreams, I have hallucinated about the magic of color, brought on by the endorphins one also experiences with orgasm, or sexual ecstasy. And here, on this magical night, I got to see the Northern Lights, not in Alaska, but on Lake Champlain in Vermont!

I truly enjoyed this assignment. Since I was still recovering from my breast-cancer surgery, it proved to be a healing place for me.

Salina, Oklahoma

On March 29, 1998, I was feeling strong again, so I accepted an assignment at the Cherokee Clinic in Salina, Oklahoma, in the northeastern part of the state. It is really quite lovely there. Driving along the superhighways (at 75 miles per hour) revealed long views of farmland and lots of big sky. I came into the western edge of the Ozark mountains where there are rolling hills and many lakes, such as TenKiller Lake, Grand Lake (which is really Lake of the Cherokees), and Hudson Lake. My accommodations were the best that I had ever had. A couple who owns a Bed and Breakfast near the clinic also owned a regular house with all the amenities, tall trees, and a dog. I stayed in the house, and it was more like home than in any other place that I had stayed.

Although this is true Cherokee country, most of it is no longer a reservation. According to one of my patients, who lives on a chicken ranch, there is a twenty-five-thousand-acre reservation nearby. The poultry business is as big here as it is in Talihina. And, of course, there are patients who have histoplasmosis, a lung disease caused by bird droppings.

One of the nearby industries is a factory where some of the patients spend long hours sewing draperies. From patients I learned that the factory had some ergonomic standards, with the workers doing regular stretching exercises at intervals during the day. I was impressed with that tidbit of information.

My first week at the clinic was extremely busy. On Tuesday, which is Diabetic Day at the clinic, I was expected to see ten patients and to take care of a ton of paperwork that had to be properly initialed and routed. These patients had previously been seen by a very experienced provider who had managed some of the most complicated diabetic cases, but some had not been seen by a full-time provider in several years; they had seen only contract providers, like me. I know that they were discouraged to see a strange face each time they came to the clinic. It was evident that each of us in the clinic had a slightly different approach to patient care. I managed to see six of them that first Tuesday and was told that I needed to "speed up a little."

I regained my confidence on Wednesday morning when it was "Pap Smear Day." I would be able to see plenty of women for that, since I had more experience in that arena. Even there, many who came in for pap smears also turned out to be diabetics or hypertensives. Almost every woman I saw was on estrogen of some sort. Every afternoon is for both walk-in acute-care patients without appointments and other patients with regularly scheduled appointments.

In this clinic, I learned what I call the "rainbow system." There were six exam rooms. Outside of each room is a set of flags: yellow, green, red, blue, white, and black. I was told what color I was to respond to each day, and when my color flag was turned out for a room, it alerted me that I had a patient inside waiting for my care. If a blue flag was out, it meant that a nurse was in there doing her thing and that I was not to go into the room until the blue flag was down. For example, if a diabetic patient was there, the nurses did a very thorough foot exam. If a pap smear was to be done, the nurse was setting up the room with all the needed equipment. The vital signs of the patient were taken in a triage area; before the patient was taken into an exam room, a white flag indicated that this was a walk-in patient. Whoever finished first with her or his scheduled patients (that is, whoever's color was not displayed outside another room) should see that patient. Because walk-ins were handled on a first-come-first-served basis, a paper attached to each walk-in's chart told you the patient's number, which was assigned according to the order in which he or she arrived.

I wanted to tell you, briefly, about how colorful a busy day can be. One day, four or five colors (providers) were working. The nurse said that whoever could get to a patient first would be just fine! Each day we had a different locum-tenens provider and a second full-time doctor and were assigned a color for that day. Dr. Teague (the chief physician) told Dr. Snelling (a young female African-American doctor) that she was black. Dr. Snelling replied, "I know I'm black!" Well, one day I was yellow, the next I was green, and I never knew what color I would be next. I was quite amused by my time with the "Rainbow System."

I want to comment on the names of the Native American patients. First, I want to say that I mention these names with no disrespect. (With a name like Jimmie Butts, I probably have no right to comment on anyone's name.) I was intrigued by seeing patients with names like Blossom, Fox, Bear, Wolf, Backwater, Dreadfulwater, Rabbit, and Hogshooter. I would trade the name "Butts" for any of those!

Dr. Teague, a Native American woman, managed the clinic well. She was kind, industrious, very smart, and expected patients to participate in their own health care. Many of the patients were diabetic and hypertensive. They knew that when they were to be seen, they had to bring all of their medicines with them. This left no doubt about what medicines the patients were supposed to be taking. Without their medicines in hand, patients will try to describe their medications: "It's a little green pill" or "You know, the big white one for my blood pressure!" So each patient arrived with a bag of prescriptions in tow. On "Diabetic Day," each was also fed a breakfast that was consistent with his or her food plan. The compliance of these patients in coming in for their appointments and bringing their medications was remarkable.

Most of the patients were on insulin, as well as pills. Many had cardiovascular disease and high blood pressure. Many had end-organ-disease—like retinopathy, kidney failure, and/or amputations—as a result of poor glucose control. Realizing the importance of diet and exercise was just not enough. The behavioral counselor told me that the worst pathology in this population was apathy. This was exactly what I had been told in Bethel, Alaska.

As I said, we saw many cases of histoplasmosis, since many locals work on the chicken farms. And there was asthma in every age group. Many of the patients take as many as twelve prescriptions a day. My patient load often exceeded my ability to be as thorough as I wanted to be while still addressing all the issues that each patient had to deal with. We saw quite a few trauma cases. Here was the first time that I had seen a woman whose cow had fallen on her. She had lacerations, swelling, and bruises on her legs, but fortunately there were no fractures.

This was also my first experience with the Cherokee tribe. They are a proud people who remember their heritage. I remembered the stories about the "Trail of Tears" in the 1830s, when the Cherokee and Creek were driven like cattle from their homes in Georgia, Alabama, and North Carolina to Oklahoma. One quarter of them died of mistreatment or neglect by U. S. soldiers during their journey, which took place in the middle of winter. They have made a life for themselves in Oklahoma, and there are many success stories.

As a child, I saw movies about "cowboys and Indians." Many of the Cherokee here are successful "cowboys" who own big ranches. Of course, like many of us who look at our heritages and find that we are descendants of a variety of cultures, there are many Cherokee who also have Irish, Scottish, or English ancestors. I have often said that, depending on my mood on any given day, I may feel more Irish (with a gift of gab) or more nomadic, since my maternal grandmother always told me that she was a descendant of Gypsies. Here the patients proudly claim their Cherokee ancestors and find both comfort and reward in celebrating their fortitude for life and the reverence for the earth that was evident in Salina.

I saw lots of children. No matter where I have worked, the children are the most receptive to an older lady with graying hair who reminds them of their grandmothers. They were very cooperative, whether I was looking in a painful ear or taking out a splinter. They were also well behaved in the reception area. Their parents were loving and firm at the same time. This was also evident in Alaska, but less so in many areas of the lower forty-eight.

I was impressed with the many artists in this area. The paintings, jewelry, pottery, and painted turkey eggs were decorated symbolically in lovely, precisely applied colors. I went to a pottery where a Cherokee man spent a good deal of time showing me around the studio and how he painted and fired his original designs on the pottery. I ordered several pieces for my daughter, Cindy, to put in her studio. She is a stained-glass artist, and her studio contains art that she has collected during her many travels. Her shop is called "Sojourner's Art." My favorite rendition on the pots or plates in the man's studio was the image of a woman in a circle, which represents mother earth. Sometimes in the images, she nurtures her baby in the curve of her breasts and belly. It made me want to nestle in her arms as well.

In Tulsa, there is an art museum called the Gilcrease Museum. Its collection includes textiles, baskets, and lovely carvings that depict Native Americans' traditions. The museum is named after Thomas Gilcrease, who was one-eighth Creek. He was brought up in what was then the Oklahoma Territory, and the allotment of land the government gave him as a Native American proved to be rich in oil. Many other Native Americans also had oil on their allotments, but in their ignorance, they often sold the oil rights to ambitious whites for a pittance. Mr. Gilcrease became intrigued with art and visited galleries in Europe and the U. S. He decided that he wanted to devote his collection to American art. He bought the best work of the famous frontier artists: George Catlin, Charles Russell, and Frederic Remington, among others. The March 1954 issue of *Life* magazine quoted Gilcrease as having said, "A man should leave a track of some sort." And the track this oil millionaire left behind is the best collection of American frontier and Native American art and literature ever assembled. The collection documents a tragic period in American history. The very names of the men in the paintings—Red Jacket, Black Hawk, Cunne Shote— echo the beat of war drums, and their stern faces show the determination and defiance that kept the North American frontier ablaze periodically for three hundred years. While Gilcrease believed that Native Americans had gotten a raw deal from the Whites, he did not want to dig up any tomahawks. He hoped his collection would give its viewers "some knowledge, some pleasure, some new thoughts" about Native Americans. Among my favorites were carvings by Willard Stone. The wood is smooth, yet shows the strength of the Native American figures in their lyrical poses. His animal figures have an almost Byzantine appearance, with their elongated necks and long legs.

A second trip to the Gilcrease Museum in Tulsa gave me the opportunity to see works by Thomas Moran and J.M.W. Turner. Moran's work took my breath away. That year, 1998, was celebrated as the centennial of Yellowstone National Park. Moran traveled out West to sketch the vast wild country. His renditions of the area in all of its glory at the turn of the century helped to secure it as America's first national park. Moran's use of light and detail in his paintings is extraordinary.

I was able to see the azaleas in bloom in Muskogee's Honor Heights Park. Some of us went to an old theater in Tulsa to see melodrama entitled *The Drunkard*. The audience did lots of hissing and booing when the villain was on stage and lots of cheering when the hero spoke. This has been one of the longest running plays in American history. At intermission they served coffee and pink or yellow sandwiches. Actually the sandwiches were ham salad or egg salad on white bread—nothing yuppie about this food! The most fun was singing along to old songs from my youth, such as "Let Me Call You Sweetheart," "By the Light of the Silvery Moon," and "When Irish Eyes Are Smiling."

I had a birthday and celebrated Easter while on this assignment. My friend, Beth Landis, who has been a traveling nurse practitioner longer than I, sent a cake to the clinic, and it was enjoyed by all. Beth had worked there before and was liked and appreciated by all of the staff. On Easter, I attended a Passion play in Tulsa at Victory Church, which meets in an auditorium on the grounds of Oral Roberts University. It was very charismatic, and the drama was intensely realistic. I was especially moved when Christ removed the bandages of two lepers and later, when he was beaten by the guards as he carried the cross to Golgotha. The violence of the act was worse than anything I had seen on television. And when he rose again from the grave, everyone cheered as if they were at an athletic event. This was a new experience for me, and I have been going to Easter pageants all of my life.

One of my patients paints turkey eggs, and he wanted to give one to me. The shell is open on one side, and there is a scene painted on the inside as well as on the outside. I cherish it because he and his wife invited me to their home to see some of his other work. I have found that kindness and a gentle humor is as healing to the patients as lab tests and prescriptions.

I left Salina with a new appreciation for Oklahoma. The area around Talihina is harsh and rocky, with little that is green or lush. I thought then how cruel it was to have sent the Native Americans to Oklahoma. Now I see that parts of it are livable and even delightful.

Rocky Boy Reservation, Box Elder, Montana

There are times when brief assignments prove to be the most fun. I was asked to work at the clinic on Rocky Boy Reservation, near Havre, Montana, during the month of June 1998. Here is where I found the most ready sense of humor among the staff and patients. This is a Chippewa-Cree Reservation, and the territory is beautiful, with rolling hills, tall grass swaying in the wind, and extraordinary beech and birch trees. It is easy to understand why the Native Americans used the long poles made from these trees to make lodges, travois for dragging their possessions, and tent poles. I truly felt that I had finally come to the West that I had only read about.

It was here that I received my "Native American name." One day I was asked what my middle initial, "K," stood for, but before I could answer, someone else replied, "Kicks." Thus, I became "Jimmie Kicks Butts." I protested, hoping that my Native American name would be something like "Passion Flower." But "Jimmie Kicks Butts" amused them and everyone I have met since. Because I am a good sport, I accepted my less-than-charming name.

There were two physicians here, both Native Americans, and one physician's assistant (PA), who had worked in North Carolina before going to Montana. All were very helpful. The PA seemed to see more patients than anyone else. As in many healthcare settings, the physicians seemed to have more administrative duties and more reasons to be away than NPs or PAs. We are the ones who stay on the front lines, so to speak. Later I learned that it was different in the Veteran's Administration (V.A.) system. V.A. doctors see an inordinate number of patients, as you will see when you read about my fall-1998 assignment.

As do all Native American clinics, this one offered a variety of services performed by the public health nurses, social workers, dentists, optometrist, and even a physical therapist who came every two weeks. Of course, it also had the ever-present laboratory, radiology, and pharmacy departments. The nurses often perform simple laboratory tests and also serve as radiology technicians. Versatility and flexibility are important characteristics of successful nurses and nursing assistants in this type of setting.

Montana is BIG! They think nothing of driving one hundred miles to get a loaf of bread or traveling even further commuting to and from work. This is where I fell in love with the "BIG SKY!" One can see for miles and miles, and the changing cloud formations prompt one to be absorbed in the clean, crisp atmosphere of this part of the universe. I have always loved our tall pines and many deciduous trees of the Southeast. I must admit, the trees do provide us with much-needed shade in the summer, but you cannot fully appreciate the vastness of the sky under the green umbrellas of North Carolina unless you escape them at the coast or on top of a mountain.

In Montana, the wheat fields are constantly moving, and the color of wheat is not just green. The sun-dappled grass takes on many hues as the breeze bends and brushes the tall stems. I asked where I could buy bread made from this wheat. I was told to go to Great Falls, one hundred miles away. Most of the people on the reservation go there regularly to buy their supplies of delicious bread. I couldn't fathom driving that far for a loaf of bread. I did go there later, on my way to Yellowstone. When I walked into the "Big Sky Bakery," it looked familiar. I asked if there was a similar store back in Raleigh, North Carolina. The clerk looked on her computer and said, "Yes, it's located in Cameron Village." I had been there many times, since it is only seven miles from my home. I had a good laugh about this.

At the clinic, many of the mothers arrived with their babies in the traditional papoose cradle, which they carried on their backs. The babies, all swaddled and tied into these colorful devices were content and were either sleeping or smiling beautifully at all who spoke to them. I never saw one baby in a papoose cradle who was fretful. And, as usual, the babies are especially beautiful.

Here I saw the usual ailments: headaches, diabetes, sexually transmitted diseases, and hypertension. There was also an epidemic of head lice underway. At that time, the public health nurses were telling patients to massage mayonnaise into their hair and leave it tied up over night before combing out their hair with fine-toothed combs to remove the nits. Head lice, like roaches and other insect infestations, have always been with us and probably will always be with us, with a new or old remedy being suggested every year.

There I saw a young woman who was having some back pain. As a child, she had had surgery at the Shriners Hospital in Oregon to correct a birth defect that had left one leg shorter than the other. By age thirty-two, some of the discrepancy in her leg lengths had returned, and by trying to accommodate this, she was putting excessive strain on her back. Both the doctor and I agreed that a referral back to the Shriners Hospital was in order. Each Indian Health clinic is allotted just so much money for the year for referral and transportation. The referral was not an issue, since she had been seen at the Shriners Hospital before, but there was no money left for transportation. And it was only six months into the fiscal year!

The patient, a bright and sprightly young woman, was not dismayed. She told me she would just hop a freight train to get to Oregon. It seems that she and many of her young friends frequently traveled around the western part of the United States in this fashion.

It made me wonder if her pain was really from this form of "exercise." We faxed the referral to Oregon, and she left with her plan to get there.

All of the nurses and support staff loved to tease me about my new name. They also teased me about my weekend adventure in Glacier Park, west of Havre.

Two of us had gone camping there one weekend at Two Medicine Campground, which surrounds Two Medicine Lake. It was lovely. We stopped at the camp store for a few supplies, and I discovered "bear bells." Because bears are most dangerous when they are surprised, some hikers wear bear bells to alert bears to their presence; most, however, are sold to tourists. Since members of my family often hike in the Great Smoky Mountains, where black bears live and roam, I bought bells for everyone, thinking it would be a novel gift.

We hiked halfway around the lake; then it started raining, and we returned to our tent to prepare supper. The ground squirrels were efficient little beggars, climbing right up on our boots to search for a morsel. The next morning, a moose scavenging in a cooled campfire hardly looked up as we peeped out of the tent.

The Piegan and Blackfeet people gave the Two Medicine area its name. The frontiersman later came through here, exploring westward. The Great Northern Railroad laid track through Marias Pass, giving greater access to the region, and Glacier National Park was established in 1910. Later came the cabins, a hotel, a dormitory and a dining hall. The camp store remains in what was originally the dining hall.

Because it was late June, the weather was cool and crisp, and it was a perfect weekend. On Wednesday, after returning to the clinic, I picked up a local newspaper. It contained a story about a grizzly bear and her two sub-adult offspring (two-year-old cubs, male and female) that had chased, killed, and partially eaten a park ranger. Glacier Park had been closed for three weeks prior to our camping trip. The adult female grizzly and her male cub had been caught and euthanized after a tribal council had authorized killing the two bears, which are sacred in the eyes of Native Americans.

The story continued. On Sunday, the third bear had "bluff-attacked" a group of hikers at the north end of the lake, just two miles from where the rain had turned us back to our tent. No one had been hurt that day, and the bear had been apprehended and euthanized. Once a bear has tasted human blood, it will often kill again. I could not believe how close we had come to being one of those hikers. Dr. Demsey, a member of the Flathead tribe, jokingly told me that a bear bell is a dinner bell and a tent is a bag lunch!

I called home to ask my husband if he had read the news. He told me that the only news he read was about our president and an intern at the White House, and he was not as impressed with my story as I was. I do find that my travel has given me more exciting stories to tell than those I usually hear back home.

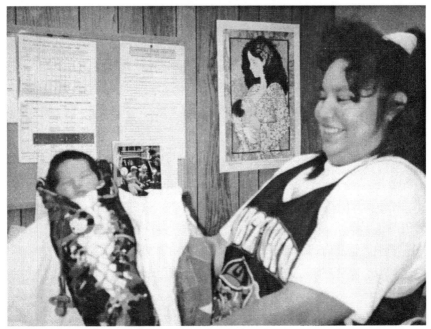

Chippewa-Cree mother and baby at Rocky Boy Clinic, Montana (1998).

Beaver Creek Park, Montana, while I was working at the Rocky Boy Reservation in Box Elder, Montana (1998).

When I finished my assignment, I traveled to see the route Lewis and Clark took when they came through the five Great Falls, and the new National Park display of artifacts representing their arduous journey was impressive. I could imagine the formidable task of portaging their dugouts and supplies. By this point in their journey, they were wearing the deer-hide shoes they had to make because the shoes with which they had begun their adventure had completely worn out.

From there, it was on to Yellowstone National Park. If you recall, in the Gilcrease Museum I had seen the marvelous paintings of Thomas Moran. He had been commissioned to document what explorers had seen in Yellowstone, and his sketches, watercolors, and his later oil paintings were instrumental in convincing Congress to declare Yellowstone a national park in 1872.

I was naive to think that Yellowstone would still look as it did in Moran's renditions. There had been major forest fires in the late eighties, and instead of millions of tall trees, we saw only their burned remains, some still standing and many lying on the forest floor. That evening we went to hear a park ranger tell us the importance of periodic fires in a forest's ecosystem. It was true that the park was alive with a rainbow of color from the wild flowers that emerged in the fires' aftermath.

My stay at Yellowstone was not as exciting as staying where the grizzlies frolicked at Two Medicine Lake. However, the moose, buffalo, antelope and all other critters were a delight. I saw Mammoth Springs, Yellowstone Cavern, and of course, Old Faithful. On the advice of my friends at Rocky Boy Clinic, I also ate Wilcoxin fudgsicles (several times!)

Leaving Yellowstone, I drove back to Billings, Montana, on Highway 221, which runs across the northwest corner of Wyoming through the most spectacular mountains that I have ever seen. I crammed a lot of sightseeing into this brief assignment, and someday I hope to return to Montana and drink in the "big sky" one more time.

Greenville, South Carolina

On October 8, 1998, I went to work at the Veteran's Administration (V.A.) Outpatient Clinic in Greenville, South Carolina. I had never worked for the V.A. and was told to expect to see about twenty patients a day. What a surprise to see the number of patients who came to this clinic each day. Even if a patient had an appointment, and most did, we saw them first come, first served. There were four teams of providers. Each team had one physician and a single nurse practitioner. These teams are color coded, and I had to learn once again what color I was so I did not pick up a chart belonging to another team. These clinics experience a volume of more than four thousand visits a month.

I saw even more pathology at the V.A. clinic than I had in Lufkin, Texas. The paperwork was voluminous. They were in the process of eliminating a great deal of paper by transferring the patient records to a computerized system. That, in itself, was enough to slow us down. We had X-ray equipment, but no radiologist, so films had to be sent to the V.A. hospital in Columbia, South Carolina for interpretation. We had no optometrist and no equipment for cleaning ears or doing minimal punch biopsies for dermatological cases. I had trouble finding a vaginal speculum when I needed to examine a woman. We sent most of the women to the V.A. Hospital in Columbia. The wait to be seen in the Greenville clinic was unbelievable. It seemed to me that it would have been more cost effective if there were enough staff or equipment to perform these procedures on site rather than having to send patients to Columbia.

Some patient stories:

- An eighty-two-year-old man with COPD (chronic obstructive pulmonary disease) and recent pneumonia had just been discharged from Stephens Hospital in Toccoa, Georgia, his hometown. His prescriptions included Zithromax and Zosyn, both powerful antibiotics. He had developed diarrhea and urinary incontinence. After evaluating his neurological signs, vital signs, lungs, heart, and abdomen, I determined that his diarrhea and incontinence were probably due to the antibiotics. His respiratory distress was in part due to the fact that he had left his oxygen tank in the car and had been sitting in the lobby for over an hour.

- I was unable to convince the doctor in Columbia that my patient needed to be hospitalized. We were able to give him a nebulizer treatment and administer some intravenous fluids before we sent him home. Later, when a nurse in Columbia asked me what I had done with my eight-two-year-old patient, I curtly responded that I had sent him home to die. I was not being sarcastic. I had discussed his eventual demise with his family. The inquisitive nurse responded that there were forms that had to be filled out to help patients plan for the "end of life." I did not mean to be impudent. However, I was not surprised to learn of forms that had to be filled out even when one is dying! Good nurses have been helping patients to die with dignity for a long time. After all, dying is a part of living, according to Forrest Gump. Helping patients to live as well as they can with disease and then allowing them to die with dignity are what health care should be about. There is not a form to be filled out that is more important than humanely caring for all individuals, whether they are patients or fellow workers. Again this is the true *art* of nursing.

A *Victory*:

To me, a "victory" was having a patient admitted to the V.A. Hospital in Columbia, the "parent hospital" of Greenville's V.A. Outpatient Clinic.

- A sixty-year-old African American man came to the clinic for his first visit complaining of numbness in his left leg. He was pleasant, cooperative, and had not seen a healthcare provider in more than thirty years. He had no pulse in the left leg. I knew that he needed Doppler studies of his blood flow and a possible ultrasound of the groin to determine if there was a blood clot. It was a struggle to get the nurses in Columbia, who schedule such diagnostic visits, to understand that they needed to make the required appointments as soon as possible. We finished his preliminary tests in a couple of days, arranged transportation, and he was eventually admitted with a blood clot that extended the full length of his leg. It was a wonder that a piece of that clot had not broken off and traveled to his lungs or brain, either of which would have caused a life-threatening situation!

- A fifty-nine-year-old man came into the clinic as a "walk-in," meaning that he did not have an appointment. He weighed only 116 pounds after having lost almost fifty pounds in the previous six months. He had not seen a doctor or sought medical help in five years. Prior to that he had been hospitalized with a bleeding ulcer, suffered complications, and wound up with a permanent colostomy. At that time he was drinking a lot of alcohol and was in serious trouble. After spending several months in the intensive care unit of a hospital, he developed terrible bedsores and these had left scars.

  I asked the patient about the possibility of exposure to AIDS, and he denied engaging in any risky behavior, including alcohol or drug consumption, since his 1993 medical crisis. He looked cachexic (near death). He was pale, weak, and his eyes bulged out of his head due to his gaunt appearance. He had on glasses and false teeth, both of which were too loose on his skull. Frankly, when I see such a patient, it occurs to me that he could lie down, die, and be covered up to go to the morgue in a matter of moments. After considering the V.A. system's rules, I knew that I must first order a battery of tests to "prove" his need for admission.

Knowing there would be a number of abnormalities, I kept him nearby, knowing that the results of his tests would begin to appear on my computer screen, highlighted as "V.A. ALERTS." This would give me enough documentation to warrant his ambulance trip to Columbia. His electrolytes—showing a potassium level of 2.7 (less than half of normal)—proved his dehydration. His hemoglobin was 7.4, when it should have been at least more than 12. The chest X-ray showed a possible mediastinal mass. More lab tests were still to come. We inserted an intravenous line, kept it open with normal saline, and administered nasal oxygen. He was admitted to the V.A. Hospital in Columbia, and although the diagnosis was grim, the patient and I were both grateful for the admission and care. A victory!

I want to talk for a minute about the personalities and ailments that typify the veterans of different wars. Each category of veterans appears to have certain characteristics that could be attributed to the time and war in which they served our country.

Many of the veterans of WW II still suffer from the effects of battle wounds, as well as from illnesses that may have existed had they never been in the service. I met men who fought with Patton and one who was present after the landing at Normandy. I met another who served in American embassies all over the world and two men who were there when Paris was liberated from the Nazis.

These men were in the seventh or eighth decades of their lives. I met one woman, eighty-two years old, who joined the woman's auxiliary in 1942, serving for twenty-five years as the Women's Auxiliary Corps (WAC) was absorbed into the regular army. After that, there was no longer a separate military organization for women. She was secretary to the commanding officer in Vietnam when she retired. She wanted to tell me the secrets that she always kept to herself, like knowing that Bill Clinton left the country to avoid the draft! (He was actually in Oxford, England, as a Rhodes scholar at that time and had a legitimate draft determent.)

Many patients who fought in Korea still suffer from illnesses connected with frostbite, as well as from battle wounds. Some had been in the antecedents of today's Special Forces, and some had come home with Korean wives. Many of these servicemen suffered from alcoholism and depression and attributed these problems to their participation in the Korean War. They did not speak of their experiences with as much pride as did the veterans of WW II. These men and women were generally in the sixth decade of their lives. Some of the women had been nurses in M.A.S.H. (Mobile Army Surgical Hospital) units, primitive, but portable hospitals located on or near battlefields.

Many veterans who came to the V.A. had never participated in actual combat. They served in places all over the globe as occupation forces, forward-placement units, or peacekeepers. For instance, after WW II, some twenty thousand armed-services personnel were stationed in and around the Middle East, with the promise of more troops that could be deployed, depending on the threat of the day. After the Korean War, more than one hundred thousand troops were stationed in Europe, serving in a variety of capacities. I had never really paid attention to the number of people who have served our country in so many ways.

The Vietnam War remains America's most controversial conflict and has left a very different mark on those who fought in that land where there were so many questions about our need to be there. Their illnesses are more often related to post-traumatic stress disorder (PTSD). The ages of the Vietnam veterans ranged from forty-five to seventy-five. There were men and women who were draftees (who were sometimes known by other monikers, such as "baby boomer" or "hippie"), career servicemen, and dedicated special-forces personnel. Not only do they suffer more frequently from hallucinations, nightmares, and "flashbacks," but they are also a population that has used more alcohol and illicit drugs than that of any other era. I wondered if this substance abuse was because of the lack of loyal, patriotic support from this nation during an unpopular war.

Then there were the young folks who had served in the Persian Gulf, in Bosnia, or other recent battles. We looked at their skin problems, their chronic rashes, their children's birth deformities, and their respiratory illnesses and wondered if those had been caused by chemical exposure, environmental factors, or germ warfare. Many of these people also have severe emotional problems. There is still a plan to screen anyone who may have ever been exposed to Agent Orange during the Vietnam War. And the waiting list is still long.

It was common to see patients in wheelchairs in the large waiting room of the clinic. Some were paraplegics or quadriplegics, many with missing limbs and some with oxygen tanks and breathing masks. Many of them, however, are just like members of other populations I have served that include large numbers of diabetics who have lost limbs due to uncontrolled blood sugar and patients who have suffered strokes brought on by high blood pressure and/or elevated cholesterol levels.

Up until 1996, most of the people who came to the V.A. for their health care were unemployed and inactive, which caused more problems with depression and physical ailments due to poor diets and unhealthy lifestyles. The V.A. was open only to veterans with "service-connected illnesses" and ailments. In 1996 any veteran would be seen, even if he or she were employed; in order to receive services, they just had to make a co-payment that was based on their financial status. With the rapid changes in America's health care, with so many uninsured citizens due to the high cost of private insurance or membership in an HMO, many were now seeking medical care in the V.A. clinics and hospitals across the nation. As a result, there were not enough providers and support staff to take care of this huge influx of new patients. On one day, we had more than one hundred walk-in patients who were willing to wait all day, if necessary, to be seen. With only four physicians and four nurse practitioners, it was difficult to see all of them. It would always take at least forty-five minutes to complete the assessment and treatment or referral if a new patient had a chronic illness as well as an acute problem.

There were days when I would see patients who were taking as many as twenty prescription drugs. By the time that I sorted through all of them, I realized that many of the patients' complaints were more related to unfavorable drug interactions than to an illness.

In one month, I saw dozens of patients with chronic pulmonary disease. Most of these have the lung problems caused by smoking. I was appalled to think that during WW II and the Korean conflict, the government provided free cigarettes to the troops. As late as the Korean War, soldiers were issued Lucky Strike cigarettes in green wrappers left over from WW II! We know how devastating nicotine addiction can be. In the clinic, there were always at least two people taking nebulizer treatments. One day when a sixty-year-old man finished his treatment, I found him outside smoking a cigarette before I could listen to his lungs again. I was outraged, and chaperoned him back into the clinic. When he returned the next week, I had to tell him that his chest X-ray had revealed a suspicious lesion in his lungs.

Those who were in alcohol and cocaine recovery swore that it was more difficult to stop smoking than to stop their other drugs.

The clinic had two psychiatrists and one psychologist, and the demand for their services was difficult to meet.

> I saw a thirty-two-year-old man whose problem was anger and hostility, which caused him to lose job after job. His wife, afraid of his outbursts, was threatening to leave him. There was no open appointment for two months, but I found an appointment for him in one month. I worried about what could happen in the meantime. For three years, he had been seen in three or four different emergency rooms with chest or stomach pain and where he had had expensive diagnostic tests done; their results assured him that he was physically well, and he was offered no further assistance. He was given emergency numbers to call at the V.A. Could that have been enough? He denied that he had any suicidal ideation at that time and said he had never hit his wife or children. His wife said this was true. His ranting and verbal abuse, however, were big problems. Looking at him and his wife, one saw an attractive young couple, both of whom appeared basically healthy, but inside, their personalities in dire crisis.

As I write this, I would like to reflect on some ideas that have come out of my experiences. It occurred to me that the limitations and controls and bureaucracy of Indian Health Service and the Veterans Administration Health Care could be eventually mimicked by Health Maintenance Organizations. God forbid that this should happen. It is no wonder to me that so many Americans are turning to alternative medicine. They fear a system that will simply write a prescription that may or may not be an acceptable formula due to its costs and/or its availability to certain socio-economic groups. The thought of this possibility in a land that is supposed to provide the finest medical care in the world sends cold chills up my spine.

Note: As of January 2003, many of the services to veterans have been discontinued. An article from The Associated Press states,

"The Veterans Affairs Department will suspend enrollment today for higher-income veterans seeking health care for non military related ailments ranging from routine care to heart disease and diabetes…. The suspension scheduled to last through 2003, goes against VA policy set in 1996 to open healthcare to nearly all veterans. The change is expected to affect about 164,000 veterans." Those veterans already enrolled will not be affected.

With the present state of our economy, our war in Iraq, and a call for support of the military, it seems to me that to reduce services to veterans is not very wise.

The Paperless Chart— Dream or Nightmare?

The Greenville V.A. Outpatient Clinic had set a goal of having all information about each patient on a computer rather than as entries on a paper chart. When I first arrived, I learned that for each patient there was a computer file called an "action profile" (AP). This computerized AP file was printed out and attached to the paper chart for each patient encounter. The AP is valuable because of the information it contains, including the two most important things to know about each patient: his or her last name and the last four digits of his or her Social Security number. The latter is also the patient's medical chart number, and it is imperative for every transaction involving the patient to show this. I am sure that some of us will never get to heaven if we do not know our identification numbers! I bought a cell phone recently, and they asked for all of my numbers except for my Medicare number.

The AP also contains information about all of a patient's appointments, referrals, and medical conditions, including which of these is considered service connected. (SC) or non-service connected (NSC). These terms refer to which current medical conditions are attributable to a veteran's injuries or illness suffered during military service (coded SC) and which are related to later illnesses and injuries (coded NSC). This designation must always be noted on each encounter form and on each prescription that is writ-ten. It makes a difference in how much a veteran must pay for a service. When I first went to the V.A. clinic, the most value that the AP had for me was to provide the blank pages where I wrote all pre-scriptions, whether for a renewal of current drugs or a new pre-scription. Of course, I constantly had to open the computer program that allowed me to see which generic drugs are on the formulary, a list that changed from day to day. The "formulary" is the list of drugs that the V.A. would allow us to prescribe, usually a generic or the least expensive drug. If circumstances were dire and only a certain prescription drug would work, we could occasionally order these more expensive drugs. Since that time, more and more insti-tutions are using a formulary system like those used by the V.A. and the Indian Health Service.

I learned in South Carolina that I had to make copies of any pre-scription that I wrote, to be kept on file for one year. This meant that during each patient visit, I had to take the time to go to a copy machine before I could send the patient to the pharmacy. Once the patient took the AP to the pharmacy, it would take three to four hours for the prescription to be filled, due to the volume of patients that were being seen on any given day. I was always concerned when an insulin-dependent diabetic (IDDM) who had come to the clinic as a "walk-in" (no scheduled appointment) waited for an hour or two to be seen and then had to wait even longer for a pre-scription to be filled. We could usually find a pack of crackers or orange juice if we knew a diabetic was there without any food. I told diabetic patients who were rescheduling their appointments to bring in all medications and to bring a lunch!

The plan was to enter our notes and consults or referrals, as well as the prescriptions and follow-up appointments, into the computer system. If you are a computer person, you might imagine that this seems an ideal way to generate a "paperless chart." However, on

Thursday and Friday of one week in November, the "system was down"! It was almost impossible for us to evaluate patients without the valuable information recorded in the computer. Most of the patients did not bring in their medicines for us to check the dates, numbers, drug, and dosage on each bottle. Of course, they may have tried to describe to us the color or size of the pills, which would have been a difficult task, since most were taking between two and twenty prescriptions, not to mention any over-the-counter medicines they might be using. When I had to chase down a *PDR* (*Physician's Desk Reference*) and compare pill colors with a patient's memory of his or her medication, I had no assurance of which pill had actually been prescribed; by then he or she would say, "Well, I saw the doctor write my pill down in that chart! Can't you read it?" (Of course, they did not realize that I did not have an old-fashioned paper chart.)

Most of the providers were already entering their notes in the computer rather than on the paper charts, so none of that information was available on the days the system was down. I could not see what the original complaint had been, the examination results, the assessment, or what plan of action had been made at the last visit. Working without adequate information made for two maddening days. Only a few of the nearly one thousand prescriptions the clinic usually filled in a day could actually be filled that Thursday and Friday. I hesitated to speculate about what would happen when Father Time rang in the year 2000 and those computer systems would truly be put to a test. (As it turned out, that was not nearly as bad as these two days in 1998 had been!)

During the previous six weeks, I had seen a lot of pathology and had made many needed immediate referrals and/or admissions. No matter whom you called or consulted with at the V.A., the first question asked was, "Last name and four"? It did not really seem to matter when you told them that the "system was down" and that some of the required information was not available.

My only thought was that clinic hours were *not the right time to add new systems*! It would have been better if the clinic were closed when the information highway was detoured for whatever reason. Even I had dreamed of a paperless chart since I first stated working at SAS Institute in 1984. But when the system is down, it is truly a nightmare!

I was privileged to observe and work with those who labor diligently to make the V.A. healthcare clinics' and hospitals' system work. It appears that this system does not have all of the advantages of private systems and is limited by government funds when it comes to hospitalization and advanced procedures. In some ways, there is a greater demand for skill at the front end of care, the care that is given to the veteran on the first visit. I must say that if our country moves into a socialized system of health care, I picture it being very much like the V.A. system. With the restrictions and costs of HMOs being what they are, I see major changes in the future.

Social Life in Greenville

What a pretty town! Running through the middle of town is a river with rocks and small waterfalls. The Peace Center for the Performing Arts is right beside the river, and there are cafés and specialty shops all along the tree-lined sidewalks. A wonderful library and art museum are within a block or two. Parking along the street does not seem to be a problem, and nearby lots accommodate any overflow. Traveling across the country reveals the demise of many center city or "downtown" areas, but in Greenville, citizens have done a good job in city planning, and it could be a model for other cities and towns.

I attended a program at the library called "Literature and Medicine: Partners in Health." The program's director asked us to list the skills and traits that we, the individuals in the audience, expect of our doctors and other healthcare providers. Imagine my surprise when, once this list was made, they showed us a *Sixty Minutes* television documentary featuring the practice of four nurse practitioners in New York City. It was evident that these four women personified all the qualities that our library class had expressed. Of course, I was doubly pleased to see the favorable story, since I, too, am a family nurse practitioner.

The University of South Carolina Medical School sponsored the program, which was taught in the Family Practice department. It reminded me of a session in The University of North Carolina

Family Practice program. Students are taken to an art museum to spend some time looking at different paintings. They are asked to write down all that they saw. It seems that this exercise is intended to enhance the students' skills in taking patient histories and performing physical examinations. In this day and age, we must gather as much information as possible, in as little time as possible, in order to make an accurate diagnosis.

I was privileged, while in Greenville, to see and hear the St. Petersburg State Symphony Orchestra. It was as if Tchaikovsky's wonderful melodies had transported me to Russia. In Mauldin, South Carolina, near Greenville, I saw a Broadway musical, *Purlie Victorious*, which is based on Ossie Davis' 1961 play, *Purlie*. The Alice Childress Theater Company (ACTco), which staged the production, is committed to Black Theater. Part of their mission statement states that they will "support and nurture the development of African American playwrights and their plays. And establish and maintain a sense of community by telling our stories, our way, therefore, promoting understanding and appreciation for our cultural differences." The cast was skilled, enthusiastic, and musically talented. For me, it was important to witness this method of enhancing the cultural heritage of this Southern state. The experience reminded me of the festivals of the Native Americans, the National Storytelling Association, where stories are told of all of the people who make up America, and other festivals that celebrate people's Irish, Greek, Hispanic, or other backgrounds. The variety of our people—with their different histories, memories, and yes, senses of humor—that make up the strength, the wisdom, and the colorfulness of America.

As I have already mentioned, in 1984 and 1985, I served on a North Carolina Legislative Committee studying healthcare costs and the future of health care. No one—hospital administrators, insurance companies, nurses, doctors, nursing homes, or legislators—accepted any responsibility for the rising costs of health care. In 1984, I started my job at SAS Institute, helping to establish an on-site Health Care Center for the employees and, eventually, their families. I was able to prove that healthcare costs did not need to be as high as they were. Preventive care and education are cost effective. Today, SAS Institute's Health Care Center has fifty-five employees, including nurse practitioners, doctors, nutritionists, psychologists, a physical therapist, a full laboratory, and a dedicated support staff. Documentation still supports the cost effectiveness of such a program. What is the future of health care in America? We have become a nation of high technology and, in some ways, a nation of greed. We want the best, we want it now, and those who have the most money and the best insurance can get it. It may sound socialistic, but the day will come when we are humbled and figure out a way to make it possible for everyone to receive the same high quality of care.

What can I, a single person in a sea of caregivers, do? I can look into the eyes of any patient I see and listen and touch and do my best. These simple acts are worth more to the patient than anything else I can offer. This is what I want from *my* caregivers: to hear my complaints, my fears, and my hopes for a healthy life. There are times when I do not have answers, but I am dedicated to finding answers for my patients and offering them everything I have to give. This is the *art of nursing*!

Morenci, Arizona

Where in Arizona? I had never heard of Morenci. Just as people often get their notions about Alaska's beauty of from travel brochures, when they think of Arizona, they think of the Grand Canyon, fancy resorts near Phoenix, the desert area around Tucson, and the Apache, Navajo, and Hopi territory in northern Arizona. I had those visions as well.

This assignment provided me with a new opportunity. Near (*very* near) the small company town of Morenci, close to Arizona's eastern border, is the largest open-pit copper mine in the United States, the Phelps Dodge mine. In fact, the town itself has been moved twice so that the company could mine underneath the old town sites. So everything—the one grocery store, the movie theater, bowling alley, bank, and of course, the clinic—looks new.

I drove more than one hundred miles to Morenci from Tucson on February 28. Again, I was fascinated by the landscape—long vistas of desert, cacti, hills, and phenomenal rock formations. There were several small towns along the way, and the last town I traveled through was Clifton. To me, it looked like a ghost town filled with old empty buildings, some almost falling down. Clifton has a colorful history. Indeed, 1983 was a memorable year in Clifton, featuring a miners' strike against the Phelps Dodge mining company and a San Francisco River flood that nearly washed away the town. In fact, I have a newspaper with photos of the flood, and there is an interesting similarity between the devastation in Clifton and that in eastern North Carolina after Hurricane Floyd hit. I will say more about Hurricane Floyd later

From Clifton, I drove up a very steep and winding road for five miles into Morenci. As is usually the case when I first arrive at a new site, my eyes were thirsty. I drank in every tree, cloud, and sign and attempted to burn the images into my brain. The most impressive part of Morenci's scenery is *rock*: rocky terrain, big rocks, little rocks, most of which are red or coppery in color. The town of Morenci appeared to have been placed in a shallow bowl. It reminded me of a village that my son would have built when he was about eight years old, making roads where he could drive his Matchbox cars and trucks. All of the buildings looked relatively new, definitely not the look of a town in the Old West. The houses were neatly laid out in rows on streets all around the outer edges of town. I spied the Morenci Healthcare Center; right next door on a higher hill was an apartment building where I would live, off and on, for the next three months. Of course, there were schools and ballparks, and lots of room to roam. Again, the most dominant feature was the *Big Sky*! There were tall poplar trees, like those you see in the Italian countryside, and some evergreens. Down in the valleys were the mighty sycamores and some oaks, but the sky dwarfed the green of these trees. When you drive out a bit into the desert, there is a lot of mesquite. Until then, I was only familiar with mesquite as it comes in a bag from the grocery store to be used in our outdoor grill back home. And of course, there was every kind of cactus that you can imagine.

I checked in at the urgent-care center where I would be working and was given the keys to my apartment in the Coronado Apartments, which I had seen on the hill. The only address that I had received was a P.O. Box number, and it was only much later that I learned the name of the street where both the apartments and the health center are located, Coronado Boulevard and Burro Alley. I am sure there was a time when only a burro could have climbed that hill.

The view made me think of an episode from my childhood. When I was a little girl, I remember staying home from school because I had the measles. I was snuggled under a colorful "counterpane" quilt. My mother read one of Robert Louis Stevenson's poems to me:

THE LAND OF COUNTERPANE

When I was sick and lay a-bed,
I had two pillows at my head,
And all my town beside me lay
To keep me happy all the day.
And sometimes for an hour or so
I watched my leaden soldiers go,
With different uniforms and drills,
Among the bedclothes, through the hills;
And sometimes sent my ships in fleets
All up and down among the sheets;
Or brought my trees and houses out,
And planted cities all about.
I was the giant great and still
That sits upon the pillow-hill,
And sees before him dale and plain,
The pleasant land of counterpane.

As I stood on top of the hill on Burro Alley, looking down on the town, I was transported to that cozy place of my youth.

If I were a person with a negative attitude (and sometimes we all have that), I would have seen only the desolation of that part of Arizona—the dust, the meager vegetation, the rape of the land to extract the copper. My years of travel have helped me develop a new sight, a new vision. I look for the silver lining—the cloud formations, even the ominous storm clouds; the thorny cactus bears beautiful flowers and nourishing fruit. I see not only the works of man, but also the work of God, a Higher Power, and find there hope for the future.

Once again, I had a new adventure before me. After settling into my tiny apartment, I gathered the tools of the trade—stethoscope, handbooks on anatomy, physiology, and pharmacology—and prepared for my first day in the urgent-care center.

Phelps Dodge Copper Mine, the "Land of Counterpane," Arizona (2000).

I walked the short distance to the center and strode into the building with the confidence I have gained during the previous six years and the experience of nursing for over forty years. It is true that we have seen many changes in medicine during my career. I often tell patients that we call it the "practice of medicine" because we are all still practicing. People, however, do not change that much. They still look to us as healthcare providers to solve their problems, ease their pain and tend to their physical and mental wounds. The majority of the patients we saw in Morenci were Hispanic; their ancestors lived in this part of Arizona when it was still part of Mexico. Once again, I found that each community develops a culture of its own. In my original quest to explore humor in various cultures, I have learned that differences in humor are more often regional than tribal, national, or racial. A location's geography and history help shape one's notions about what conditions—climatic or economic—and traditions—social or familial— stimulate humor and laughter.

In most cases, humor is more frequently expressed by a person being able to laugh at himself rather than laughing at the expense of others. There is no doubt that a stranger coming into their midst generates situations that amuse the natives. For example, I remember how I was teased in Boston because of my accent and in Rocky Mount because I disliked eating "chitlins." This type of humor is not meant to be unkind anymore than laughing when someone slips on a banana peel. It occurs when we see or hear about anything, any person, any situation that is outside our everyday routines.

The people who live and work in Morenci are passionate, caring, hard working, and have very healthy senses of humor. One of my favorite stories about Morenci is about a miner whose ear was almost completely severed by an accident with a crane:

- This thirty-year-old man had been hit in the head (and, fortunately, he *was* wearing his hardhat) by a crane moving a long piece of metal. The collision knocked his hardhat off and nearly removed his left ear in the process. As I explored the extent of his injury, I called for the physician to rescue me from the responsibility of reattaching his ear. No such luck! I was told, "You can do it!" Again I remembered the lesson I had learned from a Native Alaskan physician's assistant: the most important task was to get that wound clean.

We used two liters of normal saline to wash the damaged ear vigorously. I was concerned that the saline would come out of the other ear! That did not happen, of course, but the repair took a long time. My medical assistant was patient and most helpful. Once she asked what we wanted for lunch. The patient could not believe we were looking down into his injured ear and thinking about lunch! He was a good sport and talked throughout the procedure. After securing the injured tissue deep in his ear with sutures that would eventually dissolve, I proceeded to reattach the ear itself. Mind you, it was not completely detached, but it did open like a door that was hinged on the facial side of his head, and sewing behind his ear was a challenge.

We all got through this, and by the time we finished, we had become pretty good buddies. I looked at him and asked if his left ear had always been lower than the right. At first, he looked startled and then realized that I was teasing him. Since Morenci's open-pit mines generate an almost constant cloud of blowing dust, when my patient asked if he could play softball that evening, I gave him a resounding "No!" Because it was difficult to put a bandage behind his ear and keep it secure over his head, the last thing I wanted him to do, besides detaching the ear once again, was to get his newly repaired wound dirty.

He told me who was playing ball in the town league, and I went to watch the game that night. When I arrived, several of the urgent-care center's employees were already watching the game. Right away, one said, "Uh-oh, look who's here!" Then they pointed to the other baseball field, where I spied my patient, with his head wrapped in electrical tape, shagging balls. I walked up behind him, and when he saw me, he was not only surprised, but also somewhat chagrined as I stood there with a provoked expression, hands on my hips. He explained that his team needed him and that he was not going to play, just help out! "Young man," I said, "you come sit in the stands with me! That's the extent of your helping out."

Each day for about the next ten days, he came by the clinic daily to assure me that he was following my instructions. Remarkably, the ear stayed attached, his hearing was not affected, the sutures were removed, and all was well. His audacity, his tenacity, and humor gave us all a good laugh.

Although the urgent-care center is not designated as an emergency room, the types of patients and medical situations that we dealt with were very much like those that major emergency rooms are equipped to handle. Since Morenci is so far from any major hospital, the first line of care that the patients receive in this setting is similar to what I had witnessed in emergency rooms.

We saw patients with heart attacks, congestive heart failure, lung problems such as pneumonia, occasional pneumothorax (collapsed lung), and occasionally a lung tumor was detected on a routine X-ray of the lung. Of course, the mine generated a lot of trauma cases among those who worked with heavy or electrical equipment and those who drove the huge Komatsu dump trucks that carry the ore. My grandchildren were quite impressed when they saw a photo of their grandmother standing beside a truck that has twenty-three steps to get to the cab. The truck drivers haul rock from the open pit mines to the ore crushers; they worked twelve hours a day, seven days a week, and then have seven days off.

In 1983, the mine's management had opposed the unions and developed work schedules that suited both the owners and the workers. For years, the unions had fought to establish a forty-hour workweek and other benefits. Now the workers and owners had set their own rules. In terms of both higher productivity and wages, the schedule of twelve-hour days with seven days on and then seven days off seemed desirable for everyone. From my perspective, however, it took three to four days for the drivers to rest and recover, and they experienced some health problems they would not have had if they had been working a five-day, forty-hour workweek. Poor diet, lack of regular exercise, poor elimination habits, obesity, hemorrhoids, kidney stones (almost endemic to this dry, hot climate), and emotional stress persisted. Of course, I am of the opinion that nurses have also brought about stressful work conditions in hospitals by choosing to work twelve-hour days for higher pay and that this contributes to the current nursing shortage. I am personally against unions, though I understand how important they were to this nation in the early years to establish reasonable work hours, safe working conditions, health benefits, retirement funds, and overall fairness for the common workers. I now believe that professional organizations support workers such as nurses in favorable ways without unions. My mother was a Teamster for most of her adult life. My father-in-law was active in the postal workers union. Yet we are surely a more reasonable nation now than in the early decades of sweatshops and child labor. I do see the physical and emotional toll that twelve hour days take on nurses and mine workers. My observations of the effects of long hours and choice of shifts prompt me to state my own personal opinion about such choices. If we hired more workers and returned to the forty-hour week, would we be faced with the nursing shortage that currently exists in hospital settings? I understand that the American people like being able to negotiate for more time off and higher wages, for a variety of reasons. We all succumb to greed, more pay, more vacation time, and more flexibility. Is this the best way to enhance the health of the workers? Do the long hours of hospital personnel, doctors, nurses, and technicians put the patients at risk? Think about it.

A few other patient stories:

- A forty-two-year-old man was working with his horses on his ranch and caught his thumb in a rope, nearly losing a portion of his thumb. This was a challenging wound to repair. Once again, I learned the value of cleaning the heck out of the wound before repairing the laceration. I also learned from the local physician's assistant that it is wise to sprinkle a little sulfa powder (crystalline sulfanilamide) on the wound before dressing it. Doesn't that take you back to the early part of the century before penicillin and keflex?

- A sixty-three-year-old woman mentioned that she was having a "little chest pain." When a person with high blood pressure comes to the urgent care center with such a complaint, we are obligated to determine if this is a cardiac crisis by performing a thorough evaluation—an electrocardiogram, the correct laboratory tests, the chest X-ray, the works. All during the exam, she smiled and made small talk. I think she was a bit lonely. This Hispanic woman was pleasant and cooperative. I noticed that she had crocheted the top of her socks. I commented on the socks. She laughed and told me that she had four sons who often appropriated her socks from her laundry to use themselves. She decided to add this feminine touch to her white socks so that they would recognize that the socks belonged to their mom.

  Her tests were negative. She was not having a heart attack, and she was discharged to go home. She asked for a pair of my socks. Since my apartment was just a few feet away from the clinic, I went to get my only other pair. In a couple of weeks, she returned my socks with a lovely crocheted top on each. I think of her each time that I wear them. I had remarked to her that the next time a big strapping boy came to the clinic with crocheted socks, I would know that it was one of her sons!

- A fifty-one-year-old woman had called the rescue squad from her apartment in Clifton, the town five miles down the mountain. The paramedics arrived in a matter of minutes to find her unconscious and needing transportation to the clinic. Transporting her unconscious body on a stretcher to the ambulance was a challenge because her house was built into the side of a steep hill with more than two-dozen steps leading to the road. It turned out she had experienced a serious asthma attack and had taken more medicine than was necessary. She was revived at the clinic and cared for successfully. The point of this story is to commend the rescue workers in Morenci. The paramedics and emergency medical technicians were a tremendous asset to the clinic and the community. They worked in the urgent care center, supplementing the staff that worked there full time. When inserting an intravenous line was difficult or any procedures needed to be done to assess or treat the patients, their skills came in very handy. I cannot say enough for their presence and help. They were well-educated, skillful, and eager to help.

- The mine's team of emergency workers was also efficient and well trained. I had to laugh on one occasion when they arrived with four young workers in tow. It seems that one of them had seen a louse on a commode seat and identified the other three men who had used that facility. The emergency workers had the boys go through the showers before I examined them. They looked rather pitiful coming to the exam room in paper gowns, shoes, and hats, but were whistle clean. I had some educating to do to discuss the "emergent" nature of this discovery. Body lice are rarely an emergency. Needless to say, I found not one body louse on these freshly scrubbed bodies.

- On all occasions while I was there (except that body-lice "emergency"), the emergencies were very real and often difficult. Shortly after I arrived, one of the giant Komatsu trucks caught fire, and the driver narrowly escaped the cab without sustaining severe burns. Even though the truck was several miles away, we could see the black smoke curl into the Arizona sky as the huge tires exploded, one by one. The driver only suffered from smoke inhalation and the realization that his injuries could have been much worse.

I worked in Morenci all of March and April and then returned again in June, when I got to witness real heat exhaustion. Temperatures soared to well over 100 to 105 degrees in the valleys, where there was little breeze. I had learned that the homes did not have air conditioners as we know them. They cool homes with "swamp coolers."

- A sixty-eight-year-old man was on top of his mobile home attempting to repair his swamp cooler when he passed out. The rescue squad brought him in and the entire team went into action to cool him down with cold intravenous fluids. His body temperature was 106 degrees. He was wrapped in wet, cool blankets, and ice was packed around him. He was also a patient with hypertension and a heart condition, and in the midst of this, he had a heart attack. The experience and skill of the doctors and nurses, as well as that of the rescue team, brought him out of this heat stroke, and he was later air lifted to a hospital in Phoenix.

Each time we had a serious illness or accident, helicopter pilots and medical teams would arrive to transport and care for the patients. Unlike Alaska, where airplanes are utilized in emergency flights, here helicopters are the most efficient means of transportation. Believe me, if I were a young nurse, I would love to be a helicopter nurse. It may seem dangerous, but the rewards are tremendous.

Many of our patients would be frightened at the prospect of flying over the mountains and desert to arrive at a major hospital in Tucson or Phoenix. The skill and demeanor of the nurses, however, put them at ease and delivered them out of harm's way.

In any emergency or urgent-care setting, some patients come in and remain rather calm and quiet despite having very serious illnesses, while others who do not have serious illnesses are hysterical. How do we—as nurses, nurse practitioners, or doctors—sort out or triage who needs help first and how extensively we need to evaluate the situation? This is always a challenge.

I came to work one morning, received a report from the doctor who was ready to go off duty, and began my day.

- My first patient was a ten-year-old Hispanic boy who had been brought in by his parents about 6:00 a.m. complaining of stomach pain. A flat-plate X-ray of the abdomen had been taken, and it was determined that he was probably constipated. He had just expelled the contents of his enema when I went in to see him. He did not have a high fever, which might indicate a "hot" (infected) appendix, so a complete blood count had not been done. When I looked into his eyes, I saw pain and fear that seemed to be caused by more than just constipation. I ordered the blood work, which showed that his white blood-cell count was elevated but not as high as is generally seen for appendicitis. I called a surgeon in Safford, a town with a small hospital just seventy miles from Morenci, and we decided that he needed a surgical evaluation and that it was safe to transport him in his parents' car. About 3:00 p.m., he was seen, and the surgeon decided to perform surgery to look into his belly. His pancreas had a small laceration, and he had early stage peritonitis (infection of the entire abdomen.) and was in deep trouble. Had I asked his kind and concerned parents about possible abuse? Who had hit this child in the belly? How could this be? It turned out that the child and his older brother were fans of the World Wide Wrestling on television and were practicing some of the fighting they had witnessed. There was no harm intended, but this child nearly died.

I think watching wrestling is hazardous to one's health. At least it was in this case. Since that time, I have seen documentaries on television about teenage kids who try to emulate the moves performed by professional wrestlers and suffer some serious consequences as a result. After six weeks in the hospital on tube feeding and intravenous antibiotics, the child finally was discharged from the hospital and came home to Morenci. We were all grateful for this outcome.

In our very diverse nation, prejudice still exists. Having grown up in the South, I witnessed bigotry and injustice. My experience with African Americans was almost nil when I was a child. We could not afford to have a Black person to do our laundry or help in the yard. I always attended segregated schools, including nursing school. I had finished my diploma program and was working at the University of Tennessee Research Center and Hospital on my first real job before I worked with or took care of a Black person. I was warmed by the friendship I had made with a Black nurse in the nursery. She was bright, industrious, immaculately dressed, and was kind to me. I learned a great deal from her about her people as we sat and rocked and fed the newborn babies. The Black babies born with heads full of hair were so pretty, looking so complete already compared to the pale, often bald White babies. Later in my life, in 1969, I became a Girl Scout Leader, and parents had to call me to see if their daughter could be in my troop. Two of the girls were Black, and I was delighted to have them in my troop. I had a visit from the Girl Scout Council, who informed me that the troops in Raleigh, North Carolina, had never been integrated. The church where we were to meet did not want an integrated troop in its building. No problem for me; we met in my home over the next six years.

I am aware that many of the Native Americans in most of the places where I have worked still feel resentment about the Whites who took away their land and brought them syphilis, small pox, and alcohol. They have some distrust of anyone with blue eyes, but white hair helps because they do respect the elderly! Now, in Arizona, I learned of a new prejudice among Hispanics. Those who live and work in Morenci have some disdain for the Mexicans who illegally cross the border, crawl through the desert and do not go through the proper channels to become American citizens.

- There was a Hispanic woman in this community who assisted the illegal immigrants in any way that she could. When someone was sick or injured, she would bring him or her to the urgent-care center. One forty-year-old man had sustained a severe laceration of his leg from crawling on his belly and being scratched by one of a mesquite bush's vicious thorns. The wound became infected. Despite her first aid and loving care, it became more and more infected, to the point where the pus and gore reached down into the bone. By the time he came to see us, the leg was almost gangrenous. Despite daily care, soaks, debridement (removal of dead and damaged tissue), and antibiotics, the leg would not heal. It was time for him to see a surgeon in Safford. The logistics were complicated. An emergency Medicaid application was in order, but he was not a U.S. citizen. Somehow, everything was taken care of, and he received the care he needed and eventually healed. One Hispanic nurse expressed disdain because this illegal person received care that she thought he was not entitled to. I sometimes reflect on the origin of prejudice and look into my own soul to see if I also harbor some prejudice. I am grateful to realize that people are the same no matter what their color, facial characteristics, or mores. I am sure that I am not prejudice free. However, my insatiable curiosity about the heart, soul, and mind of man—any man, any woman or child—erases any fear, trepidation, or anguish that would cause me to back away from an encounter. I do seek understanding in regard to other people whether they are patients, co-workers, or any other citizens of the world.

There are a few other patient issues I wish to tell you about:
- A three-year-old male, who was a bundle of energy, had made a flying leap from an upper-bunk bed and caught his left upper arm on an open dresser drawer, sustaining a deep laceration. As we removed the dressing that stopped the bleeding, blood spurted out as if an artery had been severed. It was frightening, and of course, he was screaming to high heaven! Thank goodness, an orthopedic surgeon happened to be in the clinic that day to care for some miners' injuries. A nurse fetched him, and he came to my rescue, evaluated the wound, and repaired it after anesthetizing the hysterical child. No artery had been severed, just a large vein. Different specialists come to Morenci periodically, and it was his day to be there; I was grateful for this coincidence.

  The child healed nicely. Hopefully, there will be no more jumping from upper-bunk beds, but knowing the nature of an adventurous child, this will probably not be his last injury.
- A forty-three-year-old Hispanic man had been coming to the clinic for months, complaining of headaches, as well as other miscellaneous pains. His history led us to believe that he was what we call a "drug seeker," a patient who may have legitimate pain but who comes in so often in the absence of proven illness that it reminds us of the story of the child who cries "wolf" when there is none. Eventually the wolf is at the door, and no one believes the child.

Somehow, I felt that this man was having real pain. I made a decision to order more Demerol for him and had a laboratory test done that suggested anemia. I referred him to a specialist in Tucson. As it turned out, he did, indeed, have bone cancer, which causes anemia. He was grateful for the referral, even though his prognosis was grave. He sent me a lovely ceramic angel, saying he was thankful that I acknowledged his pain. In May, I returned to North Carolina, and when I went back to Morenci in June, I learned of his death. I left the little angel for the nurses who work diligently and patiently in the clinic. Maybe I wanted to remind them that things are not always as they appear on the surface.

Of course, one cannot work in Arizona without seeing a patient who has suffered a scorpion sting. I have learned that in adults this is not so severe, but when a fragile baby or elderly person is stung by a scorpion, however, the pain is devastating.

- A nine-month-old was brought in screaming at the top of his lungs, and there was only a small red lesion on his leg. The family had seen and killed the small scorpion on the sofa where he was playing. The child had to go to Safford to be hospitalized for a day just to control the pain. I never liked the look of scorpions anyway, and they seemed to be everywhere in Arizona.

Arizona Social Life

Social life in Morenci: Would you believe that I never got to the Grand Canyon nor made it north to the land of the Hopi? My initial interest in becoming a traveling nurse practitioner was inspired by Dr. Carl Hammerschlag, who worked for more than twenty-five years with the Hopi in Arizona. Arizona is a big state! My husband joined me to visit my only living aunt in Tucson, and we visited the Sonora Desert Museum and saw the famous Saguaro cactus, as well as other plant and animal inhabitants of the desert. We drove west to a Native American town that seemed deserted except for a cow walking down the main street. The highway was long and narrow, and every few miles, there were flowers to mark someone's death in a highway accident. We were curious about why there were so many accidents on a straight road. I am sure that speed and alcohol play major roles.

I visited with my Aunt Jean several times. She is my mother's baby sister and is only a few years older than me. She had lived with us for a short while during the Korean War, when her husband was in the Air Force; then she moved west many years ago, and we had a lot of catching up to do. I know so few of my mother's relatives anymore, and to travel back in time to my youth with this delightful woman was very special to me.

One weekend, I went south to Tombstone and saw a pretend "Gunfight at the O.K. Corral," which seemed very theatrical and touristy, and also stopped in Bisbee, another bonanza of tourist attractions. Originally it was a mining town. The locals do not seem to be in a hurry, and the atmosphere is best described as "laid back"! The mine here was also owned by Phelps Dodge. A railroad had been brought in by the mine's owners during its peak productivity, and in those days the mines yielded millions of pounds of copper, plus substantial quantities of gold, silver, lead, and zinc. The heyday of the mine eventually ended, prohibition closed the lively saloons, and many people moved away. Victorian houses still cling with regal dignity to the up-and-down terrain. Bisbee, at thirty-five hundred feet, escapes the punishing heat of Arizona's desert summers, and even in winter, if a snow falls, chances are it will be gone by noon. Visiting there when it was off-season for tourists was pleasant. There is much history, nostalgia, and charm in this old, old town.

While in Arizona, I visited the Gila cliff dwellings in nearby New Mexico, where Native Americans climbed up into the caves every day, bringing game, vegetables, firewood, and water to their abodes. I am sure that no one was obese. With that kind of daily physical exercise, there was a better chance of dying from an accident than from diabetes or heart disease.

The area offers ample evidence of the locals' love of horses and trail riding. Once I came upon a group of campers by the Blue River. They were the Greenlee County Sheriff's Department, practicing horseback rescue of lost hunters, hikers, etc. I was offered real cowboy coffee, made in a huge aluminum pot into whose depths an egg had been broken to settle the coffee grounds. The coffee was hot and appreciated in the coolness of the day. We were also thankful for the cook's hospitality and conversation.

Residents of the Coronado Apartments were always around to visit with in the building's piano room. One most interesting man was my next-door neighbor. Each evening I would hear marvelous piano music coming through the walls, and I soon met the pianist, Steve Hallett. He had recently been the subject of a Public Broadcasting System segment and had been interviewed and featured because he was a welder in the Phelps Dodge mine who spent his off-hours writing, composing, and recording piano tunes for sale. When he could, he played at the town's one restaurant and at a number of social events, including the one-hundredth-birthday party of *The Copper Era*, the local newspaper. What a fascinating man with his big hands and his ability to tickle the ivories to make such lovely piano music. He lived in Morenci during his work-weeks and then drove home to Phoenix (a long way!).

My social life once again was fulfilled by the friendship of my co-workers. Having a meal together, telling stories of how we came to be in Morenci, swapping clinic stories, and other long conversations give me fond memories of my stay in Arizona. Karin van Nieuwenhuizen, a physician's assistant who came originally from South Africa, was particularly helpful to me. Her husband, Tom, and their young daughter, Zoe, welcomed each and every one into their home; Jim Ragland, the medical director, and his wife Rosalee were pleasant, and it was fun to visit with them.

Once we had dinner in Clifton at a wee little café that also served as an art studio and antique store.

I met Tom Shumacher and his wife, Consuello, in Clifton. A friend of Aunt Jean's in the Tucson Presbyterian Church insisted that Tom look me up. He came to the clinic to find me, and I was invited to their home for a meal. We had a real Mexican meal and heard about the history of Clifton, including stories about the old mine, the flood, and the strike. We also learned of the best places to hike or fish. I will always remember their kind hospitality.

Becky Farrell, a nurse, invited me to stay at her parents' ranch one weekend, since they had returned to Long Island, New York, for the summer, and Becky needed someone to feed the horses and dogs. The house had once been a stagecoach stop and was full of interesting things, including her mother's art and studio. While I was there, my imagination ran rampant thinking of the history of this mysterious place. That weekend could provide a story in itself.

Ed Brown, a physician's assistant and Morenci resident, had worked in the urgent-care center for most of his career. I went to him with many questions in regard to reading X-rays, setting bones, and repairing complicated wounds. He also knew the people, the patients he had cared for so many years, as well as their families, their pets, their idiosyncrasies, and their strengths. Jeff Vaughan, a paramedic, was young but wise beyond his years. Karen Spivey, another paramedic who worked by his side, taught me a great deal about emergency work. Spending three months in this small town, however, provided opportunities professionally and socially that I had not experienced to this extent before. If given the opportunity to return to Morenci, I would be sorely tempted, even though I decided to stop traveling in September 2000. The mine workers were also helpful and seemed appreciative for all that was done at the clinic and in the urgent-care center. A safety manager, Syd Garay, gave me a tour of the mine, and later I was able to take care of him on one or two occasions (a motorcycle accident and then a bit of atrial fibrillation). In a small town, there are no secrets.

On weekends, I always had the opportunity to take a long walk or drive north, south, or any other direction. North of Morenci was a rather treacherous road that wound through the mountains of the Apache Reservation. It is not a road that I wanted to ride on after dark. Yet the scenery was terrific, with lots of large trees and high cliffs.

While in Morenci, I was having dinner with Karin and her family one night and suffered the pain of a kidney stone. Needless to say, I was well cared for. When I returned to North Carolina, I had it removed surgically in July. It seems that everyone who lives in that dry climate gets a kidney stone sooner or later, especially if one does not drink enough water!

- I had the privilege of taking care of Hal T. Ward, a writer for The Copper Era. His heart rate had dropped to about thirty-eight beats per minute, and we had a battle on our hands getting him to take a helicopter flight to Phoenix to get a pacemaker. He was planning a huge reception at the paper's office in Clifton to celebrate one hundred years of publication. He did not think that he could depend on anyone else to get the invitations out. Well, he went, after we talked to a woman who agreed to get the work done, and as a result, I was invited to the celebration. What a treat to be with the folks who had survived the flood and the strike of 1983.

The Copper Strike of 1983 brought national attention to the area. In Morenci and Clifton, strikes had occurred against the Phelps Dodge mine on several occasions. This one lasted almost three years. Families were split over the controversy, and some violence occurred. Some workers would cross the picket line to enrage those who demanded they stay away and be true to the strike.

In the midst of this strife and economic challenge, another event occurred. The San Francisco River, which runs through Clifton, surged over its banks in October 1983. This was the worst flood ever to hit Clifton; the river uprooted huge cottonwood trees above the town and carried them downstream, forming dams, and its floodwaters reached out to destroy all nearby buildings and houses. Fortunately, the flood occurred in the daytime, and no lives were lost. The evidence of this damage is still present twenty years later. The families who were in dissension over the copper strike came together to face this new trauma. They seemed to forget their differences and pitched in to help flood victims

As I travel, live, and work in some remote pockets of this country, I am impressed with how the history of each area affects the personalities of the inhabitants. The residents of Clifton are resilient, determined, and loyal to the land. As for their humor, it seems to bubble up at interesting times and during some very serious situations. Once again, my "accent" and my name were a source of fun for those with whom I worked. And it is just fine with me if a person feels comfortable enough to tease me and we can laugh together.

Hurricane Floyd,
September 1999

"You had to be there!"

We knew it was the season, early September. Dennis was the first real threat, with his temperamental nature, coming close then staying put, but not going away. Then Floyd came to the East Coast. I had joked a few years back when they started giving male names to hurricanes. That first year no storm with a male name ever got to shore because men do not usually stop and ask for directions.

Floyd was no joke. He meant business. However, the rain and windstorms that came after were the real threat. After Dennis, we had six to eight inches of rain from the Coast to the Piedmont (the central part of North Carolina.) This rain fell fast and hard and hit the arid ground after a long drought. The rain ran off but much of it soaked the roots of our huge trees, which still had all their leaves. When the rain and wind of Floyd came, the trees were uprooted, and the rivers swelled. That caused a remarkable flood situation.

I read the papers. I was saddened for the people of Turkey, Greece, and Taiwan, who had suffered through earthquakes that same year. I listened to the news and thought I could grasp the impact of Floyd on our neighbors to the south and east. I was wrong. This was truly a case in which one "really had to be there!" I was asked to join a cadre of nurses who were heading for

Greenville, North Carolina, to relieve local nurses who had been in the shelters working day and night for three to four days.

We met in an administrative building in our state's capital city, Raleigh, where the staffs of all of the emergency operations— Federal Emergency Management Agency (FEMA), Red Cross, and Public Health Services—were present in great numbers and as busy as bees answering phones, meeting, and putting together plans of action. There were eleven of us nurses from Raleigh, Cary, Robbins, Pittsboro, Chapel Hill, and other places across the state. The hardest part for us was to hurry up and then to wait. We waited for our assignments, our transportation, and as much instruction as they would give us. We were to relieve those exhausted nurses in five shelters around Greenville.

North Carolina is accustomed to hurricanes, their damage and their effect on the people in the areas of destruction, damage, distress, and chaos. Once we had arrived by van at Pitt Memorial Hospital in Greenville, we received our individual assignments. The hospital was experiencing electrical failures and was running on generators. The city water was polluted, and administering care was a challenge.

Four of us flew in National Guard helicopters across the Tar River to the shelters that were not accessible by land. Another adventure for this old lady! We were strapped in, given earplugs to reduce the deafening noise of the copter, and told to hold on to our backpacks as we rode to our designated areas with the doors open. Yes, it seemed a thrill until I began to see the devastation below me: church steeples rising up through the water, floating cars, pink pigs on top of barns, and rooftops floating from the houses they once covered.

My nursing partner and I went to the Wellcome Middle School shelter. Unless someone had a cellular phone, our only contact with the outside world was by radio. Of course, since there was no electrical power, those cell phones could not be recharged.

Excited to ride a Blackhawk helicopter until we saw the devastation of Hurricane Floyd in eastern North Carolina (1999).

The U.S. Marine Corp used small planes to fly-in supplies, while helicopters and trucks (where roads and bridges were open) brought in food and clothing from nearby communities More than four hundred flood victims were being sheltered in this school, and every moment, others arrived who needed medical attention. This site had been designated to triage the clients who were quite ill or had "sensitive needs." A doctor from Pitt County Hospital was there, as were a number of nurses, social workers, and few Red Cross volunteers.

The volunteers included people who dispensed meals (of course, there was no way to cook a meal!) and high school students who entertained the many children being sheltered there. Others were sorting donated clothes by size and arranging them for families to pick out what they needed at designated times during the day.

There were showers, and water was running, but it was already contaminated. Later, bucket brigades were formed so that rainwater could be used to flush commodes. Most people were sleeping on the floor, with blankets or sleeping bags as their beds. We had a few mattresses and cots for those who were ill. I have never been in a war zone, but I could imagine the frustration experienced by a newly formed M.A.S.H. unit.

We immediately went to work seeing patients. All of those who had open wounds and had walked in the floodwaters needed tetanus shots. After four days, many who had chronic diseases had run out of their medications, and even if they had not lost their motor vehicles to the flood, they could not get to a pharmacy because of the swollen Tar River.

The nurses provided first-aid care and evaluated the medical complaints. In the thirty-six hours that I was there, we sent about seven patients to the hospital in Greenville by helicopter.

- One was an eleven-year-old boy, a cerebral palsy patient with a fever of 103. Another was an eight-year-old girl with cerebral palsy who had four or five seizures while in the shelter. She was vomiting, and one of the nurses was able to create a rectal tube from some intravenous tubing so that we could administer oral Valium rectally. We had some IV fluids and administered them to a fair number of people. However, we would not have an otoscope to look into ears for another twenty-four hours and were treating people rather empirically on the basis of symptoms that we could hear and partially observe.

There were many diabetic patients whose sugar was too high, hypertensive patients whose blood pressure was too high, and many asthma patients. The Wellcome Middle School shelter had a fair number of over-the-counter medications, as well as emergency drugs and a few prescription drugs from Pitt Memorial Hospital. We were able to treat many of the patients. Later I learned that the Wellcome Middle School had been designated as a medical shelter and that there were a doctor and some supplies present at all times. Other shelters had limited medical supplies or none at all.

You may have heard relief workers refer to these clients as victims or even refugees. The term "refugee" was not far wrong in this case. By the time we returned home, we looked a bit like refugees ourselves; we had to borrow dry socks, shirts, and jackets, since the weather had suddenly turned cold. One nurse said, "You, too, could look like a refugee. Come work at a shelter."

There are many stories to be told, but the best I heard were the following two: Two nurses were sent to North Pitt High School shelter, where there were 830 refugees. One of them went to another school, Stokes Elementary, which had only had about twenty refugees at that time, and the other Public Health nurse stayed at North Pitt. At Stokes, there were no supplies, not even a thermometer! The nurse decided that she needed to know the potential problems that she might be confronted with when two hundred people were transferred to Stokes. She asked a volunteer who lived nearby to get her yarn in a variety of colors. She interviewed the clients and color-coded each of them according to her diagnosis. If they had hypertension, she put a red piece of yarn on their fingers, diabetics got green, pregnant women had navy blue, etc. She decided if someone passed out, she would at least know the treatment possibilities. I thought this was extremely creative.

The Public Health nurse who was assigned to North Pitt high School had to be most creative when running water was no longer available. There was an abundance of rainwater. She formed a bucket brigade of people to bring water into the school to flush the commodes. They used a phrase to describe the rules for flushing: "If it's yellow, let it mellow! If it's brown, flush it down!" The sanitation situation was getting much worse, however. She decided to move her people to a nearby shelter in Bethel, where running water was still available. At this time, the local sheriff asked her about a possible "riot" that occurred in North Pitt the night before. She

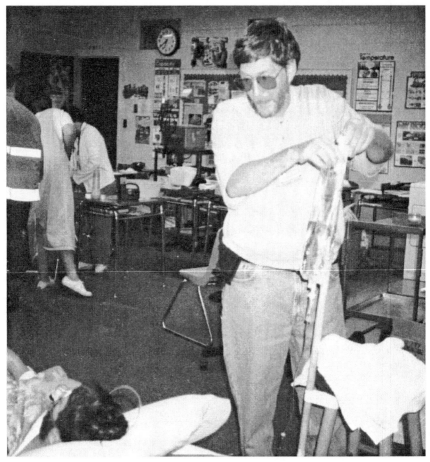

*Using a broom handle as an IV pole at a shelter following the floods
from Hurricane Floyd in North Carolina (1999).*

explained, "There was no riot, just an altercation between two
teenagers." He told her she could not move the people to Bethel
until he had a chance to investigate. At that, she replied, "We are
moving, and we are moving now!" "Who are you?" he asked. She
replied with authority "I am a *Public Health nurse!*" At that point
the move started and was completed in short order.

There were many heroes in this disaster: the National Guard,
the pilots of medical and army helicopters, the hundreds of volunteers who sorted clothes and served food, the nurses, the doctors,

and other health personnel. A pharmacist came from Bethel to see how he could help obtain some of the drugs that our patients with chronic disease required. The Pitt Memorial Hospital staff did a fantastic job administering the assignments, etc.

The real heroes were those people who had lost everything yet pitched in to help at each shelter. A young woman who had been helping at the Wellcome Middle School shelter since the first day was sitting beside me in the Blackhawk helicopter as we returned to Greenville. She saw for the first time the neighborhoods, the airport, the planes, and the cars that were covered by the cresting river. She gave an audible gasp and covered her mouth in shock at the devastation of her homeland. All that I could do was touch her, and she knew that I understood the feelings that were filling her heart and mind at that time. These people were the real heroes. The courage and spirit of those who realize that they must start building their lives all over again provided the energy that helps one to get through such events.

Yes, as I said, I had read of the earthquakes in Turkey, Greece and Taiwan. But sometimes you just have to be there to understand the true meaning of disaster.

Working with FEMA

I had a call from Washington, D.C., asking if I could establish a temporary clinic to care for the Federal Emergency Management Agency (FEMA) workers while they were working in North Carolina during the Hurricane Floyd disaster. So what was it like working for FEMA? First of all, most of those working were people my age. Those of us who were retired (and, in my case, I use the term lightly!) had each filled out an application listing our skills and experience and expressing our interest in working in some capacity when disaster struck.

Of course, my nursing experience was needed in this situation. FEMA workers would be in North Carolina for more than two months. Many had their own medical problems. All of those who would go into the flooded areas needed immunizations, tetanus shots, influenza shots, and hepatitis-A vaccinations. One man was bitten badly by a dog when he tried to enter a home to assess the damage. He was taken to a nearby clinic for stitches but needed aftercare when he returned to his home base in Raleigh. Each morning I applied fresh dressings, made sure no infection set in, and later removed his stitches.

I learned much about what needed to be done. One couple was responsible for identifying caskets that had floated up out of cemeteries, and they were making plans to have them reburied. Dead pigs, goats, and other farm-animal carcasses had to be disposed of safely. Damage assessment was a serious issue when it came time to compensate the victims. Many of the FEMA workers were full-time employees who understood all of the politics and financial arrangements that were required to work toward a resolution. By the end of December, more and more of the disaster-recovery responsibilities were being directed to North Carolina state officials, and my services were no longer needed. I learned a great deal, and despite the tragedy of this hurricane, it was a meaningful experience. Some of the busiest employees were the psychologists and counselors.

Imagine this: Each day, I wake and go to the bathroom, use the toilet, take a shower, and brush my teeth. My electric refrigerator is well stocked with food. My gas stove stands ready for me to cook, not to mention the microwave, toaster, and coffeemaker. I tidy up the kitchen, leave for work in my car that takes a road with no obstacles other than the usual heavy flow of traffic. I take all of this for granted. Once you have worked with the victims of a flood where all this is gone, you soon realize the many comforts you have.

Rocky Mount, North Carolina

In the summer of 1995, I had a number of short assignments. At one clinic in Rocky Mount, North Carolina, most of the patients were insured by Medicare or Medicaid. The staff and nurses at Oakwood Clinic were excellent. For the most part, they had been loyal employees for a number of years. But, as with many clinics across the country, there is constant change. They learned that the practice was soon to be bought-out by a large organization, and everyone became anxious about the clinic's future: Where would their patients receive care? Would the employees' jobs be secure? Whether you work for a healthcare organization, a power company, a telephone company, or a computer-related business, you should recognize this anxiety. As I write this in 2002, there are more buy-outs, lay-offs, and reorganizations than I remember in my lifetime.

I was privileged to work in the Oakwood Clinic on two or three occasions over the years. There were usually four providers—two doctors and two physician's assistants and/or nurse practitioners with over one hundred patients on the daily schedule. The day started at 8:00 a.m. and lasted until 5:00 p.m. We did have an hour for lunch, the patient flow was efficient, and the nurses were very helpful. The work here was very similar to what I had done when I was a new nurse practitioner caring for mostly indigent patients.

In a practice of this sort, many of the patients have serious chronic diseases such as diabetes, hypertension, cardiovascular conditions, and lung problems. It is difficult to see them, take a good history, do an adequate physical examination, and make the appropriate decisions regarding any needed prescriptions, teaching, and referrals. Of course, with a brief assignment, I do not know the patients at all. And I needed to design a way that I could do well (provide a safe practice of medicine) in a short period of time. I decided to find a new way of taking patient histories. For example, one seventy-two-year-old woman had diabetes, hypertension, and arthritis. When she came in, I asked her about her day. Where did she live, in a house by herself or an apartment? Who else lived with her? Was she caring for young children, grandchildren, or others? Who did the grocery shopping? Who brought her to the doctor? How did she manage to pay for and take all of the medicines that we prescribed? I learned far more about how she managed her life and her illness than I would have by using a more conventional question-and-answer method. I realized that this is truly an art and not a science. The results were favorable for the patient and for me in caring for her. It was a friendly visit that acknowledged the challenges of her existence, her courage, and the happiness or meaning that she found in life.

The children in this clinic were fascinating. Just as I saw among the Native Alaskans during my Bethel experience, children are very important to African Americans, and a strong sense of family prevails. I have also learned that certain cultures are more supportive of the elderly and show much respect and a very willing spirit in caring for the extended family. It seems that those of us who are better off tend to place our elderly parents in institutions other than our own homes. And our homes are much more spacious than those of these other, more caring cultures. When I say "cultures," I also include those who have a strong religious faith, especially those for whom respect for the elderly is important in their faith.

Children provided much of the humor that I experienced in this setting. I still carried my magic coloring book, magic scarves, and soap bubbles to capture their surprise and laughter. When you are comfortable with a child, you also gain the respect of a parent.

When Hurricane Floyd came to eastern North Carolina, there were many disruptions, and many areas were flooded. Although few lives were lost, many homes, businesses, livestock, and whole towns were wiped out. Rocky Mount was profoundly affected by the flood. Newspaper stories about natural disasters may affect you. But once you have been to a place and met the people who live there, you feel a different sense of empathy or sympathy for them. After the flood, I could not rest until I learned whether or not the clinic was still intact and everyone was okay. Many of the employees' homes were affected. In June 2001, more than a year and a half after the disaster, some were just moving into their new homes.

As for my social life in Rocky Mount, it was as limited as my stay. In every place I visit, however, I like to try some of the local food. I mentioned earlier that I was teased about eating this often-unusual food. A cafeteria in town was noted for its "soul food." For the first time in my life, I saw chitterlings—or "chitlins" as everyone calls them in the South—on the buffet. I know, of course, that chitterlings are part of a pig's intestines, but I decided to try them anyway. I tried them, but I don't think I will eat them again. They were really pretty bland, but my mind may have played a few tricks on me. Of course, I was teased a lot about that experience. I have learned that when you are a stranger or a visitor in someone's territory and you are enthusiastic or just plain nosy, people are amused to see you try your wings with the local culture—in this case, food that is a regional treat, like the stinkfish in Alaska. The locals just sit back and watch your reaction, and if you are a good sport, it provides them with a good laugh.

Nowata Clinic, Bartlesville, Oklahoma

In October 1999, I was working for FEMA in Raleigh after Hurricane Floyd. However, I had committed to work in the Nowata Clinic in Bartlesville, Oklahoma, with the Cherokee tribe for two weeks and left to fulfill that contract. This clinic was quite different from the Cherokee clinic in Salina. At the Nowata Clinic, two physicians alternated workdays, and the clinic also had a new mobile unit that traveled north of Nowata to see patients who had transportation problems. It was a busy clinic. Each of us saw between twenty and thirty patients a day. I was allowed a great deal of autonomy and even worked there by myself on a couple of days

I was happy to be able to contact Dr. Gloria Teague, with whom I had worked in Salina, at Tahlequah, where she was currently acting medical director. She had been helpful to me while I was in Salina, and I was comfortable calling her for advice on one or two occasions. The standards of care for diabetics we had used in Salina were also being followed in this clinic, and we had many diabetic patients, as well as a substantial number of cardiac patients. The nurses at the Nowata Clinic were very helpful, as were the other support staff. Without them, I could not have kept up with the volume of patients.

As in all of my assignments with Native Americans, I learned that the support staff knows much about the patients that is not recorded in their medical records. The staff knows the families, the work that they do (or their lack of it), and the patients' strengths and weaknesses. When I speak of the "art of nursing," this is where it happens. From the time a patient calls for an appointment, the staff swings into action to prepare me (and the patient) to assess his or her needs and make a plan for care and recovery.

My most interesting case at the Nowata Clinic involved a family of five—husband, wife, and three children—all of whom had Von Willehands disease.

When I was a nurse-practitioner student, I learned that if I looked at the skin of a newborn and saw more than five café-au-lait spots, I should be concerned about the possibility of this disease. Even my own youngest daughter had three of these spots when she was born. A café-au-lait spot is just what its name suggests: an irregular brown area that is the color of coffee with cream. Von Willehands disease involves a serious complication—rampant growth of tumors all over the body, both inside and out.

- The father had become completely disabled by the large number of tumors this disease had caused. They and their associated growths covered his entire body. He had had many of the tumors removed that affected his spine and other areas that interfered with his lifestyle and health. He and his family lived in a trailer down by the river and literally camped out all the time.

  I saw his three-year old daughter, who had suffered severe burns on both of her feet when she walked barefoot in the dying embers of their campfire. Fortunately, with daily debridement (removal of dead and damaged tissue), regular changes of dressings, and a course of antibiotics, the burns healed nicely. The young heal better than those of us who are older.

Not all of our patients were poor. Many lived comfortable lives with good homes, worked in jobs that provided more than enough financial support, and made major contributions to the community. As I did in every public health facility, I saw folks from both ends of the socio-economic spectrum.

There was much to see in the community around Bartlesville. Will Rogers' home and a museum chronicling his life and accomplishments are in nearby Claremore. You may recall that the story of Will Rogers' last flight to Alaska, which ended in his death when the plane crashed, had affected me with some trepidation as I prepared to leave on my first assignment.

I am continually intrigued by Cherokee names like Blossom, Littlehawk, Hogshooter, Bear, Panther, Wolf, Bluebird, Black Bear, Back Water, Buzzard, and River. Every name has a meaning, and I was eager to hear the personal stories behind them, yet the assignment was brief, and I needed to return to my post in Raleigh to care for the FEMA workers.

Choctaw Indian Hospital

Talihina, Oklahoma, January 2000

I had last been in Talihina in January 1996. What a change the healthcare system had undergone since then! Under the direction of a new tribal chief and a new board of trustees, the first tribally owned hospital in the country had been built. This was one of many good decisions that have been made to improve the delivery of health care to the Native American population. When I worked there before, referring patients to another hospital or to any kind of specialist medical facilities had been complicated and occasionally required a patient to travel great distances.

The new hospital has made it possible for specialists to come to Talihina and staff the facility's special clinics. Cardiologists, orthopedic physicians, dentists, psychiatrists, and other specialists are now available right in the hospital. This efficiently designed hospital is well cared for. The tribe's pride is evident in everything one sees there. The new obstetric department is lovely and has all of the state-of-the-art amenities.

I was asked to work in the outpatient pediatric clinic. Dr. Sarfo, who was originally from Africa, was my supervising physician. He still had a strong accent that many of the patients could not understand. They sensed, however, his caring spirit and wise counsel. I also learned a great deal from him about pediatric care. Once again, the nurses and support staff helped to make my job easier. In fact, many of the nurses whom I had met in Talihina in 1996 were still there and seemed quite happy to be a part of this innovative plan. When I had last worked there, the hospital was drying up because of poor financial management, hospital bed space was decreasing, and staff were being laid-off daily.

I had the opportunity to attend a hospital board meeting, and the Choctaw Tribal Council was in attendance. During a discussion of hiring practices, it became clear that the Tribal Council wanted to hire more Native American nurses and doctors. Members of the tribe who had returned to the area after medical or nursing school were treated like royalty. In my opinion, this seems like the right thing to do. No matter how bright or caring someone like me could be, we cannot be as effective as one of their own.

The patients received me well, and the work was pleasant. In the clinic, we saw a lot of childhood illnesses, including infectious diseases, ear infections, bronchitis, and asthma; of course, we also performed well-child care. I was privileged to spend three after-noons a week in Hartshorne, a nearby town where Jones Academy, a residential school for Native American children, is located. The children, ages six to eighteen, live there for a number of reasons. Originally it was an orphanage, but as is the case with many orphanages around the country, many current residents are not truly orphans. One or both parents of most are still alive, but for what-ever reason, are not able to care adequately for their children. Some of the children have behavioral problems, and many come from families that just do not have enough money to take care of them.

For some time, the registered nurse who worked there was the most stable and regular employee who took care of the children. The physician's assistant, nurse practitioner, or doctor were, like me, temporary contractors working as the main healthcare providers for the kids. Therefore, because there was no full-time provider, the registered nurse and the kids saw a constantly chang-ing array of faces.

The illnesses I saw there ranged from the usual acne, bumps and bruises, and lacerations to more serious conditions, such as upper-respiratory diseases, anxiety, and depression. The Jones Academy was not a part of the Choctaw Indian Hospital System at that time. The registered nurse, Melita Homer, had worked there faithfully for more than seven years. She did a great deal of counseling on smoking cessation, sexuality issues, alcohol and drug abuse, and other problems that sometimes occur when children come from dysfunctional families. The counselors who worked there were wonderful, but were sometimes overwhelmed. Ms. Homer longed for a regular provider who would have the same interest in the children that she had. In the absence of a regular provider, it seemed very easy to miss illnesses such as endocrine or orthopedic disorders.

I wrote a letter to the Choctaw chief and the Tribal Council pleading with them to help Jones Academy employ a full- or part-time regular provider, even if only for twenty hours a week. I will honestly say that this is one of the few times that I would have considered taking such a position. This experience was truly a highlight of my long career. I never had a complete answer to the problem, yet I felt comfortable saying my piece.

If any one child or student left the academy with a positive outlook, good health, and hope for the future, it would be golden. I am sure that there have been some. After several weeks there, I was somewhat dismayed that many of those who were eighteen to twenty years old were skeptical about the future they would face when they entered the world outside the gates of the campus. It would be good if the Choctaw nation and their former peers honored, in some way, those who succeeded after leaving the academy.

The children did not attend their classes on campus. They attended the local schools and sometimes experienced social ostracism by the "town" kids. The plan in 2000 was to once again provide an on-campus academic program for the first time in forty-eight years.

In the February issue of *Bishnik*, the official publication of the Choctaw Nation of Oklahoma, Brad Spears, the Administrator of the school said, "By reinstating a school at Jones Academy, we will be in a position to fully meet the needs of our Native American students." Delton Coxe, the tribe's treasurer and a former administrator of Jones Academy said, "Hartshorne has served our kids well, but it's time for us to resume responsibility of the education of our children. The Choctaw Nation now has the ability and capability of doing it well."

When I first drove up to the campus, I saw a strange sight—kids out walking pigs. It seems that some students are given a pig to care for and to enter into the local Future Farmers of America competition. The pigs were clean and well cared for and were a source of pride for those responsible for their care. I was amused to think of city kids taking a pig for a walk!

As to hospital news:

Gary Batton, Executive Director of Health, wrote an article in the official newsletter of the Choctaw Nation Health Services Authority, *Choc-Talk*. During the first year of operation in the new facility, he said, "We do offer more services than a lot of people in the United States are privileged to having... with these new services, we have grown from approximately 140,000 patient contacts to more than 200,000 patient contacts. In each clinic, we are creating between 75 and 150 new charts per month... Last but not least is our accomplishment of receiving an 84 on our JCAHO survey." Every hospital in the country strives toward the Joint College Academy of Hospital Organization's (JCAHO's) approval and certification. The hospital's score represented a major accomplishment.

Just as in every other area in which I have worked, there is always something humorous. A young physician's-assistant (PA) student from Tulsa was working at the pediatric clinic as part of her clinical rotation. These students were housed near the old tuberculosis hospital, which was falling down in disrepair. Even in 1996, when I had been there before, I was told stories of ghosts and strange events that occurred in that old stone building. The PA student was staying in one of the stone cottages near the building that housed the recovering alcoholics. She was an attractive blonde and got some wolf whistles and lots of looks from the young men. She also heard sounds and creepy music and was sure that her cottage was haunted. We shouldn't have teased her, but we couldn't help it. Security was looking out for her, so we didn't worry too much about her safety.

One day, however, I was sitting near the entrance to the hospital's clinic area. For some reason, the automatic door started opening and closing, even though no one was there to trigger the action. At first, I was puzzled and then amused when I thought that perhaps a ghost from the old hospital was paying us a visit.

As for the social life in Talihina, well, it was limited, but I appreciated taking long walks and trips to Tulsa. I would go back, given the opportunity. I did connect with some old acquaintances that I had made during my previous trips to Oklahoma for lunch dates and picnics, and I visited more Native American courthouses and landmarks. I love Native American pottery and paintings and went to Tulsa to visit the Greenwood Cultural Center and the Indian Arts Festival. The storytellers and fancy dancers always inspire me to know more about the Native Americans' heritage.

I also was able to take a side trip to Eureka Springs, Arkansas, before flying out of Fort Smith to return to North Carolina. A friend and I had a wonderful stay in an interesting bed-and-breakfast and were invited to a party the evening that we were there. Eureka Springs is very artsy and eclectic. In some ways, Eureka Springs reminded me of Gatlinburg, Tennessee, with its many shops, and stirred my memories of many vacations retreats there when it was more rustic and not so touristy.

Returning to Oklahoma is almost like going home to Tennessee, where all of my family roots remain. Going to visit my husband's family in Hartsville, Tennessee, to the lovely hills by the Cumberland River, or to Nashville to visit other family members—the areas where we both finished high school, where we were married, and started our life together—makes me feel nostalgic. After five assignments in Oklahoma, it is comforting to reconnect with old friends and see the changes that have taken place. Just as North Carolina is known for hurricanes and storms, Oklahoma has had more than its share of tornadoes. Every book set in Oklahoma that I have read contains tales of hiding in a cellar and battening down the hatches while a tornado rips through the country. It makes me think of Oklahoma as wild, unpredictable country. And yes, I would (and did) return.

Tishomingo, Oklahoma

On July 1, 2000, I flew into Oklahoma City to drive on to Tishomingo, where I was to work for a short time in the clinic of the Chickasaw Nation Health System. This was a part of Oklahoma that I had not seen before and a tribe with which I had no familiarity. And it proved to be a treat. I only stayed for three weeks but packed a lot of work and play into this, my last locum-tenens assignment.

Tishomingo—I do love the musical sound of Native American names. Just saying the words transports my spirit to the West, the plains, the pueblos, the mountains, the United States before the White man came. I often look at photographs of my great grandparents, Mammy and Pappy Brock, and see Cherokee characteristics in their faces and imagine that I have some Native American blood, as well as the Scotch Irish of the Kennedys, my father's people, or the European characteristics of my mother's people. I wrote an article once regarding my desire to be a "wanna be." Wherever I go and whomever I meet, I imagine that I have some kinship with these people and want to be like them, to understand them, to be included, to feel the pain and the joy experienced by people of all colors and cultures. I suppose that, besides having a natural desire to travel, I have a natural desire to be like a chameleon and integrate myself completely into each new environment.

Now I have come to the land of the Chickasaw. Tishomingo was the last of the Chickasaw war chiefs before the tribe left its homelands in the East. He died along the way in 1838. When the Chickasaw separated from the Choctaw to form their own nation in 1856, they honored Tishomingo by naming their capital Tishomingo City. The Chickasaw were traditionally a people of great courage. Tishomingo, Oklahoma, still reflects the influence of these people in its capitol building and in the tribe's healthcare system.

In my quest to discover the humor in various people, I truly found the most ready senses of humor in this place. (I do not forget, however, the humor of the Chippewa-Cree in Montana!) Dr. Elaine Wills, the chief physician, greeted me and introduced me to patients as Jimmie Kicks Butts, hoping the name would intimidate them and motivate them to take better control of their diabetes or other ailments. The nurses followed suit and would tease me (and the patients) in friendly ways.

Each nurse, administrative or auxiliary staff member was quick to assist me and show me the ropes while I was learning how to take care of this special group of people. Many of the patients were

Staff at Chickasaw Clinic in Tishomingo, Oklahoma (2000).

severe diabetics, and keeping their blood sugar in control was quite a challenge. Besides those with regularly scheduled appointments, there were many walk-in patients to be seen each day. Does all of this sound familiar?

Dr. Wills expressed confidence in me whether I was applying a needed cast, surgically removing a lesion, or performing procedures she ordinarily enjoyed doing herself. This crowd loved to eat, and took any occasion—a birthday, a holiday, or just a food day— to bring in delectable dishes and to celebrate. (I find this to be true in many places where I have worked. No matter what stresses there may be, one of the solutions is to have a potluck lunch.)

- One of my favorite patients (I suppose that I should not say "favorite," but it is true) was a ninety-year-old Chickasaw woman who came in for her usual appointment to have her diabetes evaluated. She was immaculate in her grooming and presence. I asked if there were any problems she wanted to discuss. Since I was a woman, she told me about a persistent rash on her upper thighs and allowed me to see it. (She had seen a male nurse practitioner the last few visits and did not want to tell him about the rash.) It proved to be a fungal rash that we cleared up with some Lotrimin. Yes, it was a simple problem, but her modesty kept her from mentioning it for some months. What was remarkable about this lovely woman was that she lived alone and took excellent care of herself, despite the fact that she was totally blind. Family members checked on her, brought her to the doctor, and took her to the grocery store and to church. I told her that I was privileged to have met her. What a good example of independence and grace she set for all of us.

Other patient stories:
- One man had a broken arm; this was complicated by a laceration that had been surgically repaired, but was still healing

underneath the cast: I became a bit more skilled at removing the cast, dressing his wound, and making a new cast that could be easily removed to tend the wound.

- Another sixty-year-old gentleman came in for the third time with chest pains. A careful work-up had been done, but it showed no evidence of a heart problem. I sat with him and asked if he was depressed. As it turned out, he had been reassigned in his job at a railroad station. For years, he had held the same job, checking arrival and departure times and for any possible problems in the station; he had a wonderful work history—so wonderful, in fact, that he was promoted to do a job that required him to use a computer. He did not feel he could possibly perform these duties. Since there were only a few months until he could receive full retirement, Dr. Wills and I were able to secure him a medical leave while we treated his depression. I do not know if he received his full retirement. I think about those of us who have been good employees for so many years and then must learn new skills. Most of the time, things work out. We have training and practice that assists us in our new roles. It is not, however, always easy to shift gears after twenty or thirty years doing the same job.

- Most people have "skin tags" somewhere under their arms, on their necks, or under their breasts. One young woman had the most remarkable skin tag I've ever seen. It was located under her arm and was about two inches long, thick, and had a warty appearance. Dr. Wills told me to remove it, which I did without difficulty. Then I was to cauterize the incision. I had never used a cautery before. Dr. Wills taught me how and encouraged me to be more aggressive despite the smoke I smelled during the procedure. Biopsy proved the young woman's skin tag to be a benign lesion, but it was an ugly thing, and the young woman was delighted to have it removed.

Two nurse practitioners worked at the clinic. One was away on maternity leave, and that was the reason I was asked to work here for a few weeks. The other was Israel Aunka. He, like Dr. Wills, was Native American. Another nurse midwife came in a couple of days a week to see pregnant ladies and perform gynecological care. It was a well-run clinic. Once again the nurses were delightful and helpful.

Social Life in Tishomingo

It was *hot* in Tishomingo! Temperatures soared above 100 degrees many days in August. And unlike Arizona, the humidity was high; this was not my kind of weather. Dr. Wills seldom had someone to play golf with, and I had given up the game several years ago for a number of reasons. But she talked me into a nine-hole game, promising to take care of me if I had a heatstroke.

There is a small, nine-hole course near town, and we took off late one afternoon. One reason I had given up golf was the challenge of water holes. Besides a river that ran next to the course, there were no ponds or water holes! This was promising. I was also accustomed to "rough" consisting of trees, weeds, and rocks. The rough on this course was simply tall grass. This, too, seemed promising. I learned, however, that losing a ball in that tall grass was more of a challenge than I expected. I drank water faithfully, but by the sixth hole, the temperature had reached 105, and I really wanted to quit. We managed to finish, and I actually had fun.

In 1994, when I worked on the tundra in Alaska, my husband came to visit. He loves to play golf. He was a bit surprised to find a golf course built on the tundra; the "course" consisted of nine rubber airplane tires, with a tin cup in the center of each. The tires were spaced apart pretty well, but it is almost impossible to walk on the tundra's soft turf, much less hit a golf ball off of it. The local pilots had designed this course because they really missed the game. But when it comes to golf courses, there is really no place like home (in North Carolina).

As for the rest of my social life in Tishomingo: I was fortunate to stay in a lovely bed-and-breakfast, The Club House Inn, owned by Joette Corbin, a wonderful cook. She also owned a funeral home. Before I met her, I had never known the many facets of funeral-home ownership. She should write a book. Joette handled a number of funerals during my short stay in Tishomingo. She would be all dressed up, but her duties included everything from transporting a body, sometimes from many miles away, to fixing a broken commode. We had some interesting conversations. One evening we went to a play at a nearby dinner theater to see Shakespeare's *Two Gentlemen of Verona*. I was pleasantly surprised to find such an event in this area of the country.

Other nearby attractions included Fort Washita Military Park in Durant, Oklahoma. Under the Indian Removal Act of 1830, the Five Civilized Tribes were taken from their eastern homes to lands in the West. The Chickasaw were the last of the Five Tribes to be moved. They began their journey west in 1837, headed for the western and central portions of the land given to the Choctaw in 1830. Their new home extended from Arkansas west to the one hundredth meridian and north from the Red River to the Canadian and Arkansas Rivers. Here the Chickasaw were attacked by Plains Indians, who lived to the west, and by the Texas Militia. The militia would often cross the Red River in search of raiders, venting their anger on any Indian who came into view. To protect the Chickasaw, the federal government established Fort Washita.

In October 1841, after his survey of the Choctaw and Chickasaw lands, General Zachary Taylor recommended that the new fort be established in the south-central part of the district on the Washita River. Fort Washita was to house a number of different groups. Many companies from different branches of the army were stationed at Fort Washita in the years before the Civil War. In addition to dragoons and infantry, several companies of U.S. riflemen, light artillery, and cavalry were garrisoned at the post at different times. Many of the commanding officers of these companies would later distinguish themselves during the Civil War on both sides. With the outbreak of the Civil War in 1861, Fort Washita was abandoned by federal troops and occupied by Texas Confederates. The War Department regained control of Fort Washita at the end of the Civil War, but frontier expansion had made it obsolete as a military post. In 1870, it was transferred to the Department of the Interior, which later turned it over to the Colbert family, members of the Chickasaw Nation. In 1962, the Oklahoma Historical Society decided to reconstruct the barracks. The fort also houses a museum and the preserved remains of several pre-Civil War military buildings that present a unique picture of military life in the Old West.

Among the other places I saw was Lake Texoma, south of Tishomingo. The landscape of western Oklahoma, part of the plains that stretch up to the Rocky Mountains, is very different from the Choctaw country in the southeastern part of the state. I also drove to the town of Gene Autry, Oklahoma, which is no bigger than a train stop, but I had a good lunch at a political rally in the Gene Autry Museum, where stories of his life and times were everywhere. Of course, many politicians were friendly and solicited my vote until they learned I was from North Carolina.

Epilogue

"There is a healing spirit in the world more powerful than any darkness we may encounter. We sometimes lose sight of its force when there is too much suffering and too much pain. Then suddenly the spirit will emerge through the lives of ordinary people who hear a call and answer in extraordinary ways."

MOTHER TERESA

Now it is time to say farewell to the wonderful people I have met, and to take with me the stories, the history, and the warmth of my seven years on the road. Will I be a better nurse as a result of my experiences? Will I be a better person? No matter what the answer, I would not trade my adventures for anything, and I am grateful for having had the opportunity to experience them.

When I began this adventure, I was in search of humor in various settings. I have learned that differences in humor are more often regional than tribal, national, or racial. A location's geography and history, the climate, economics, traditions help shape one's notions about what there is to be taken seriously or what makes us laugh. Social and family structure and style also stimulate humor and laughter.

In 1982, I developed an educational event for twenty psychologists in Butner, North Carolina. Here we have a federal institute for prisoners with psychological problems. Working there is a tough job. Part of the program was to find out what these twenty men, who worked in similar institutions across the country, laughed about, what they found humorous now, and to look at the history of their lives and think of laughter around the supper table. Of the group, only five remembered laughter at mealtime! As they worked in small groups, it became evident that humor had not been a part of the young lives of the majority of these PhD psychologists. The workshop was for one day only. I had my work cut out for me.

As the day progressed, the men began to look inside themselves and discover that humor is possible even though self-control, discipline, and decorum (Webster says that "Loud laughter in the library shows a lack of decorum.") do not allow one to "cut loose," to express emotions that are spontaneous and even euphoric. Humor does not have to be unkind, does not have to poke fun at others. Humor is a way of opening yourself to others in positive ways. It has been said that humor is more of you, only in reverse. For some, revealing one's self seems risky and makes one vulnerable.

In all of my workshops, I have quoted Herb True, the author of *Humor Power*, who has given me permission to use the following words:

Humor is a quality which can evoke mirth, cause merriment, or entertain in a pleasurable way.

A sense of humor is the ability to recognize and express humor.

Humor power is the art of using your sense of humor, and applying humor, to improve your relationships with others and your straightforward evaluation of yourself.

Those are words I try to live by.

As I wrote in the "Introduction," I hope my experiences have shown you that connecting with people by listening, touching, laughing, and caring, with your eyes, ears, and heart can make a difference. When you do, the rewards are priceless. As I said, I am no Mother Teresa. I have been paid for my endeavors, but my real rewards go far beyond a mere paycheck. They will be with me forever, when I remember the twinkle in the eyes of the aged and the wonder in the eyes of a child.

It was suggested that I tell you more about my experience with breast cancer. It was painful, depressing and scary. I am one of the lucky ones, however. I am doing well and grieve for those who had a far more devastating experience than mine. I also salute the courage of those who are still in treatment. For me, it was a blip on the radar screen of my life. I just keep on going; like Satchel Page said, "Don't look back, it may be a'gainin' on you!" I do not like to talk about it very much. I think I am experiencing what is called the "survivor syndrome." Deep in my heart and mind, I ask why am I still here when I have lost so many friends to this dread disease. I cannot explain my feelings.

But I know that God is not finished with me yet. And all of you, in whatever capacity you live and work, are each a work in progress.

Go for it!